# Contents

D1377910

2018 Cumulative Supplement to

# Arrest, Search, and Investigation in North Carolina

Jeffrey B. Welty and Christopher Tyner

UNC | SCHOOL OF GOVERNMENT

The School of Government at the University of North Carolina at Chapel Hill works to improve the lives of North Carolinians by engaging in practical scholarship that helps public officials and citizens understand and improve state and local government. Established in 1931 as the Institute of Government, the School provides educational, advisory, and research services for state and local governments. The School of Government is also home to a nationally ranked Master of Public Administration program, the North Carolina Judicial College, and specialized centers focused on community and economic development, information technology, and environmental finance.

As the largest university-based local government training, advisory, and research organization in the United States, the School of Government offers up to 200 courses, webinars, and specialized conferences for more than 12,000 public officials each year. In addition, faculty members annually publish approximately 50 books, manuals, reports, articles, bulletins, and other print and online content related to state and local government. The School also produces the *Daily Bulletin Online* each day the General Assembly is in session, reporting on activities for members of the legislature and others who need to follow the course of legislation.

Operating support for the School of Government's programs and activities comes from many sources, including state appropriations, local government membership dues, private contributions, publication sales, course fees, and service contracts.

Visit sog.unc.edu or call 919.966.5381 for more information on the School's courses, publications, programs, and services.

Michael R. Smith, DEAN
Thomas H. Thornburg, SENIOR ASSOCIATE DEAN
Jen Willis, ASSOCIATE DEAN FOR DEVELOPMENT
Michael Vollmer, ASSOCIATE DEAN FOR ADMINISTRATION

FACULTY

Whitney Afonso
Trey Allen
Gregory S. Allison
David N. Ammons
Ann M. Anderson
Maureen Berner
Mark F. Botts
Anita R. Brown-Graham
Peg Carlson
Leisha DeHart-Davis
Shea Riggsbee Denning
Sara DePasquale
James C. Drennan
Richard D. Ducker
Jacquelyn Greene

Norma Houston
Cheryl Daniels Howell
Jeffrey A. Hughes
Willow S. Jacobson
Robert P. Joyce
Diane M. Juffras
Dona G. Lewandowski
Adam Lovelady
James M. Markham
Christopher B. McLaughlin
Kara A. Millonzi
Jill D. Moore
Jonathan Q. Morgan
Ricardo S. Morse
C. Tyler Mulligan

Kimberly L. Nelson
David W. Owens
William C. Rivenbark
Dale J. Roenigk
John Rubin
Jessica Smith
Meredith Smith
Carl W. Stenberg III
John B. Stephens
Charles Szypszak
Shannon H. Tufts
Aimee N. Wall
Jeffrey B. Welty
Richard B. Whisnant

© 2018
School of Government
The University of North Carolina at Chapel Hill
First edition 1986. Fifth edition 2016.

Use of this publication for commercial purposes or without acknowledgment of its source is prohibited. Reproducing, distributing, or otherwise making available to a non-purchaser the entire publication, or a substantial portion of it, without express permission, is prohibited.

Printed in the United States of America

23 22 21 20 19      2 3 4 5 6

978-1-56011-936-4

Chapter 5

# Interrogation and Confessions, Lineups and Other Identification Procedures, and Undercover Officers and Informants    55

# Preface

This supplement updates the fifth edition of *Arrest, Search, and Investigation in North Carolina* (UNC School of Government, 2016), written by former School faculty member Robert L. Farb. The supplement includes cases from the United States Supreme Court and from North Carolina's appellate courts, plus North Carolina legislation.

The supplement is current through July 1, 2018. It therefore encompasses all decisions from the October Term 2017 of the United States Supreme Court. It also includes all pertinent legislation from the 2017 and 2018 sessions of the North Carolina General Assembly, though the legislature may reconvene at the end of calendar year 2018, after the publication of this supplement.

This supplement does not include any content relating to two chapters of the main volume. Chapter 1 (An Introduction to Constitutional Law and North Carolina Criminal Law and Procedure) contains general material about the structure of our legal system, and those broad principles have not changed since the fifth edition was published. Chapter 6 (Rules of Evidence in Criminal Cases) is a relatively short chapter and, for most readers, a secondary focus of the book. Therefore, we concentrated our efforts on updating Chapters 2 through 5, which together comprise the overwhelming majority of the text.

We owe a great debt to Bob Farb, not only for writing the main volume to which this supplement relates, but also for volunteering to review drafts of the supplement itself. Many of the case summaries in this supplement were prepared by, or are based on summaries prepared by, Jessie Smith. We also appreciate the contributions of the many School of Government colleagues who reviewed, edited, and otherwise improved this supplement. Any remaining errors are, of course, only our responsibility.

We welcome comments about the structure or content of this supplement, or of the main volume. We may be reached at welty@sog.unc.edu and ctyner@sog.unc.edu, respectively.

Jeff Welty
Christopher Tyner
Chapel Hill
October 2018

# Law of Arrest and Investigative Stops

## Jurisdiction (page 14)

## Limits on Law Enforcement Officers' Jurisdiction (page 14)

### *Territorial Jurisdiction* (page 14)

#### Company police officers (page 15)

Legislation enacted in 2017[1] amended Section 6 of Chapter 74E of the North Carolina General Statutes (hereinafter G.S.) by adding two new subsections. One of the new subsections permits company police agencies to enter into mutual aid agreements with municipalities and counties to the same extent as a municipal police department pursuant to Chapter 160A of the General Statutes.[2] The other permits all company police officers to provide temporary assistance to a law enforcement agency at the request of that agency, or the head of the agency's designee, regardless of whether a mutual aid agreement is in place.[3] While providing temporary assistance to a law enforcement agency, the statute provides that a company police officer has the same powers vested in law enforcement officers of the agency asking for assistance, but that nothing in the statute expands a company police officer's authority to initiate or conduct an independent investigation into violations of criminal laws outside the scope of the company police officer's subject matter or territorial jurisdiction.[4]

### *Expanded Jurisdiction through Cooperating Law Enforcement Agencies* (page 24)

Legislation enacted in 2018[5] amended G.S. 160A-288 and G.S. 160A-288.2 to create, in the legislation's words, "a presumption that allows one law enforcement agency to easily assist another law enforcement agency whenever necessary." Under amended G.S. 160A-288, the head of any law enforcement agency may temporarily provide assistance to another agency in enforcing North Carolina law if such assistance is requested in writing by the head of the requesting agency, unless doing so is specifically prohibited or limited by an officially adopted ordinance of the city or county of the assisting agency. Such assistance may include allowing officers of the assisting agency to work temporarily with officers of the requesting agency and lending equipment and supplies. Amended G.S. 160A-288.2 allows assistance to be provided by a local law enforcement agency to a state law enforcement agency under analogous circumstances. Prior to the 2018 legislative amendments, each statute stated that such assistance could be provided "in accordance with rules, policies, or guidelines" adopted by the city or county of the assisting agency.

---

1. S.L. 2017-57, § 17.2.(a).
2. G.S. 74E-6(h).
3. G.S. 74E-6(i).
4. *Id.*
5. S.L. 2018-87.

## Legal Standards (page 26)

### Introduction (page 26)

The fifth paragraph of this section of the main text discusses the wide variety of interactions officers have with people and, among other things, explains that officers do not seize a person merely by approaching him or her in a public place and asking questions if the person is willing to answer. In *State v. Wilson*,[6] the North Carolina Court of Appeals held that no seizure occurred when an officer went to a residence to find a man subject to outstanding arrest warrants and waved his hands to tell the driver of a pickup truck leaving the residence to stop so that the officer could ask the driver about the man subject to the outstanding warrants. The officer had no suspicion that the driver was the man subject to the warrants or that the driver was engaged in criminal activity; the officer did not have his weapon drawn and had not activated the lights or siren on his patrol car nor used it to block the road. When the defendant stopped the vehicle, the officer almost immediately smelled an odor of alcohol from inside the vehicle. After the defendant admitted that he had been drinking, the officer arrested the defendant for impaired driving. The court held that because a reasonable person would have felt free to decline the officer's request to stop, no seizure occurred; rather, the encounter was a consensual one. The North Carolina Supreme Court affirmed this ruling on appeal.[7]

The same paragraph of the main text explains that a formal arrest for a criminal offense clearly is a Fourth Amendment seizure. The North Carolina Court of Appeals also has held that a seizure occurs, at least in some circumstances, when an officer takes a publicly intoxicated person to jail for the purpose of assisting the person pursuant to the authority of G.S. 122C-303.[8] That statute authorizes an officer to "assist an individual found intoxicated in a public place by directing or transporting that individual to a city or county jail," but provides that such assistance may be rendered only "if the intoxicated individual is apparently in need of and apparently unable to provide for himself food, clothing, or shelter but is not apparently in need of immediate medical care and if no other facility is readily available to receive him."[9] In *State v. Burwell*, the court stated that "taking an individual to jail under [G.S. 122C-303] against his will constitutes an arrest,"[10] but seemed to suggest that an arrest would not occur if the requirements of the statute were otherwise satisfied and the intoxicated person consented to being taken to jail.[11]

### Footnote 101 (page 26)

Additional cases for this footnote: State v. Turnage, ___ N.C. App. ___, ___ S.E.2d ___, 2018 WL 2207325 (May 15, 2018) (the trial court erred by concluding that a seizure occurred when a detective activated his blue lights upon encountering a van that was stopped in the middle of the road for unknown reasons and that fled as the detective approached the van; the court of appeals explained that the defendant, who was driving the van, did not yield to the detective's show of authority until she discontinued fleeing and her further movement was prevented by an officer's patrol vehicle used to block the van at an intersection; because the defendant was not seized upon activation of the blue lights, the defendant's criminal activity observed by the detective between the activation of the blue lights and the conclusion of the chase justified the defendant's arrest), *temp. stay allowed*, ___ N.C. ___, 814 S.E.2d 459 (2018); State v. Mangum, ___ N.C. App. ___, 795 S.E.2d 106 (2016) (because the defendant did not stop his vehicle when an officer activated his blue lights and bumped his siren, circumstances that the officer observed between the activation of the blue lights and the time when the defen-

---

6. ___ N.C. App. ___, 793 S.E.2d 737 (2016), *aff'd per curiam*, 370 N.C. 389 (2017).

7. For a discussion of *Wilson*, see Shea Denning, State v. Wilson: *Was the Defendant Seized When He Stopped Upon the Officer's Signal?*, UNC Sch. of Gov't: N.C. Crim. L. Blog (Dec. 14, 2016), https://www.sog.unc.edu/blogs/nc-criminal-law/state-v-wilson-was-defendant-seized-when-he-stopped-upon-officer%E2%80%99s-signal.

8. State v. Burwell, ___ N.C. ___, 808 S.E.2d 583 (2017); Davis v. Town of Southern Pines, 116 N.C. App. 663 (1994).

9. G.S. 122C-303.

10. ___ N.C. at ___, 808 S.E.2d at 592. The court of appeals stated the same principle in *Davis*, 116 N.C. App. at 671.

11. *Burwell*, ___ N.C. at ___, 808 S.E.2d at 592.

dant stopped his vehicle were properly considered by the trial court in its reasonable suspicion inquiry; the court noted that the defendant's failure to yield to the officer's show of authority for two minutes was itself a circumstance that added to the suspicion of criminal activity).[12]

**Officer's Objectively Reasonable Mistake of Fact or Law in Determining Reasonable Suspicion or Probable Cause** (page 28)

In *State v. Eldridge*,[13] the North Carolina Court of Appeals held that an officer's mistake of law was not objectively reasonable and, consequently, a traffic stop based upon that mistake of law was not supported by reasonable suspicion. In *Eldridge*, an officer stopped a vehicle registered in Tennessee for driving without a mirror on the driver's side of the vehicle based on his genuine but mistaken belief that G.S. 20-126(b), which requires such a mirror on vehicles registered in North Carolina, applied to the defendant's vehicle. This case provided the court of appeals its first opportunity to apply *Heien v. North Carolina*, a case discussed in the main text. Reviewing the application of *Heien* in other jurisdictions, the court stated that those cases "establish that in order for an officer's mistake of law while enforcing a statute to be objectively reasonable, the statute at issue must be ambiguous."[14] The court also noted that some courts in other jurisdictions "have further required that there be an absence of settled caselaw interpreting the statute at issue in order for the officer's mistake of law to be deemed objectively reasonable."[15] Distinguishing G.S. 20-126(b) from the statute at issue in *Heien*, the court said that the text of G.S. 20-126(b) is "clear and unambiguous" and, thus, "a reasonable officer reading this statute would understand the requirement that a vehicle be equipped with a driver's side exterior mirror does not apply to vehicles that—like Defendant's vehicle—are registered in another state."[16] Because the officer's mistake of law was not objectively reasonable, the stop was not supported by reasonable suspicion.[17]

# The Authority to Make an Investigative Stop: Reasonable Suspicion (page 29)

## Determination of Reasonable Suspicion (page 30)

The final paragraph of this section of the main text discusses common misunderstandings about the legal grounds to make investigative stops of drivers for motor vehicle violations. In *State v. Johnson*,[18] the North Carolina Supreme Court took time to correct what it saw as a misunderstanding in the court of appeals opinion regarding the grounds for making a traffic stop and explicitly emphasized an inherent and invariable quality of reasonable suspicion implicit in the main text and relevant court opinions—that reasonable suspicion is a standard less stringent than a legal certainty. The court explained that while observing an actual traffic

---

12. For a discussion of *Turnage*, see Shea Denning, State v. Turnage *and Determining When a Defendant is Seized*, UNC SCH. OF GOV'T: N.C. CRIM. L. BLOG (May 23, 2018), https://www.sog.unc.edu/blogs/nc-criminal-law/state-v-turnage-and-determining-when-defendant-seized. For a discussion of *Mangum*, see Bob Farb, *When Does a Seizure Occur When an Officer's Vehicle Displays Emergency Lights That Direct a Vehicle to Stop?*, UNC SCH. OF GOV'T: N.C. CRIM. L. BLOG (Mar. 28, 2017), https://nccriminallaw.sog.unc.edu/seizure-occur-officers-vehicle-displays-emergency-lights-directs-vehicle-stop/.

13. ___ N.C. App. ___, 790 S.E.2d 740 (2016).

14. *Id.* at ___, 790 S.E.2d at 743.

15. *Id.* at ___, 790 S.E.2d at 744.

16. *Id.*

17. For a discussion of *Eldridge*, see Bob Farb, *An Officer's Reasonable Mistake of Law and Recent Court of Appeals Ruling*, UNC SCH. OF GOV'T: N.C. CRIM. L. BLOG (Sept. 27, 2016), https://nccriminallaw.sog.unc.edu/officers-reasonable-mistake-law-recent-court-appeals-ruling/.

18. 370 N.C. 32 (2017).

violation is a sufficient basis for a stop,[19] such an observation is not necessary and "[t]o meet the reasonable suspicion standard, it is enough for the officer to *reasonably believe* that a driver has violated the law."[20]

### *Appellate Court Cases on Reasonable Suspicion* (page 31)

The first case discussed in this section of the main text is *Navarette v. California*,[21] in which the United States Supreme Court held that an officer had reasonable suspicion to stop a vehicle based on a 911 call reporting dangerous driving. On page 107 of the appendix case summaries relevant to this section of the main text is a summary of *State v. Blankenship*,[22] a pre-*Navarette* case also involving a 911 call of dangerous driving leading to a vehicle stop. A recent case from the North Carolina Court of Appeals in the same vein as *Navarette* and *Blankenship* is *State v. Walker*.[23] In *Walker*, the court of appeals held that an informant–driver's tip relayed to highway patrol dispatch and thereafter to a state trooper reporting that another driver was driving danger-ously while drinking a beer did not provide reasonable suspicion to stop the defendant. The non-anonymous informant–driver reported that another driver traveling along U.S. 258 was driving at speeds of approximately 80–100 m.p.h., was drinking a beer, was driving "very erratically," and almost ran the informant off the road "a few times." At some point, though it was unclear whether before or after the stop was initiated, the vehicle in question was described as a "gray Ford passenger vehicle."[24] Noting that the informant–driver was unable to specifically identify the vehicle in question because it was out of sight and that the trooper did not corroborate the tip by witnessing any erratic driving similar to that described by the informant, the court held that the tip "did not have enough indicia of credibility to create reasonable suspicion for the Trooper to stop Defendant's vehicle."[25] It appears that the informant–driver's inability to specifically identify the vehicle in question, a fac-tor that distinguishes the case from *Navarette*, had significant influence on the *Walker* court's determination that the stop was not supported by reasonable suspicion.

In *State v. Nicholson*,[26] the North Carolina Supreme Court, reversing the court of appeals, held that reason-able suspicion supported an officer's investigative stop of the defendant. While on patrol at 4:00 a.m., an officer encountered a car parked in a turn lane next to a gas station with its headlights on but no turn signal blinking. Upon pulling his patrol vehicle next to the stopped car, the officer observed two men in the car, one in the driver's seat and the other, the defendant, sitting directly behind him in the back seat. The defendant appeared to be pulling a mask over his face but pushed it back up when he saw the officer. The officer asked the men, who said they were brothers, whether they were okay; each said yes, but the driver made a hand motion at his neck area. The officer then parked at the gas station and continued to observe the car, which did not move or display a turn signal. The officer then approached the car again. As he approached, the defendant exited the car and the driver began edging the car forward. The officer again asked if everything was okay, and though the driver again said yes, he shook his head "no." As the officer asked again about the situation, the driver interjected that everything was fine but that he had to get to work and the officer told him to go. After the

---

19. For recent cases illustrating this point, see *State v. Sutton*, ___ N.C. App. ___, ___ S.E.2d ___, 2018 WL 2625844 (June 5, 2018) (explaining that when an officer actually observes a traffic violation, it is a "bright line rule" that an officer may conduct a stop on the basis of that observation), and *State v. Jones*, ___ N.C. App. ___, 813 S.E.2d 668 (2018) (an officer's observation of a single instance of a vehicle crossing the double yellow centerline in violation of state motor vehicle law provided reasonable suspicion to support a traffic stop). For a discussion of *Sutton* and *Jones*, see Shea Denning, *A Bright Line Rule for Traffic Stops*, UNC Sch. of Gov't: N.C. Crim. L. Blog (June 20, 2018), https://nccriminallaw.sog.unc.edu/a-bright-line-rule-for-traffic-stops/.

20. *Johnson*, 370 N.C. at 38 (emphasis in original).

21. 134 S. Ct. 1683 (2014).

22. 230 N.C. App. 113 (2013).

23. ___ N.C. App. ___, 806 S.E.2d 326 (2017).

24. *Id.* at ___, 806 S.E.2d at 328.

25. *Id.* at ___, 806 S.E.2d at 332.

26. ___ N.C. ___, 813 S.E.2d 840 (2018).

driver left, the officer asked the defendant, who wanted to walk to the gas station, to "hang tight" and asked if he had any weapons. Taking account of the totality of the circumstances, the court determined that reasonable suspicion supported the officer's seizure of the defendant by asking him to "hang tight" and asking whether he had weapons. According to the court, the facts "strongly suggested that [the driver] had been under threat from defendant, as well as the possibility that defendant was in the process of robbing [the driver]."[27] Finding that the court of appeals placed undue weight on the officer's subjective interpretation of the facts, the supreme court emphasized that the reasonable suspicion analysis is an objective inquiry.

## The Authority to Arrest: Probable Cause (page 39)

### Determination of Probable Cause with or without an Arrest Warrant (page 40)

#### *Appellate Court Cases on Probable Cause* (page 41)

In *District of Columbia v. Wesby*,[28] the United States Supreme Court reversed the D.C. Circuit and held that officers had probable cause to arrest several people for the offense of unauthorized entry where the officers discovered the people at a raucous party at an unoccupied house. Officers responding to a noise complaint regarding a house that the caller said had been vacant for several months immediately observed that the interior of the house was in disarray and looked like a vacant property. The officers smelled marijuana and observed beer bottles and cups of liquor on the floor. There was hardly any furniture in the house, and the living room appeared to have been converted into a makeshift strip club. Several women giving lap dances while partygoers looked on were wearing only bras and thongs, with cash tucked into their garter belts. Some partygoers scattered upon seeing the uniformed officers. A naked woman and several men were found in an upstairs bedroom with a bare mattress on the floor and multiple open condom wrappers. Many partygoers claimed they were invited to the house to attend a bachelor party, but no one could identify the bachelor. Officers eventually spoke to a person on the phone who claimed that she was renting the house and had given her permission for the party, but officers thereafter spoke to the owner of the house who said that a rental agreement had not been reached and that no one had permission to use the house. The officers then arrested 21 partygoers for unlawful entry. Stating that the D.C. Circuit engaged in an "excessively technical dissection" of the factors relevant to probable cause, the Supreme Court faulted the lower panel for conducting an analysis that viewed each fact in isolation and dismissed individual circumstances susceptible of innocent explanation. Citing its precedents, the Court explained that a proper analysis of probable cause requires consideration of "the whole picture" and the "degree of suspicion" attached to particular acts that are suspicious even if not themselves criminal offenses. Under this analysis, the Court found that "[t]he circumstances here certainly suggested criminal activity"[29] and provided probable cause for the arrests.

### Pretextual Arrest, Investigative Stop, or Search (page 44)

The main text explains that under *United States v. Whren*,[30] an officer may make an arrest or conduct a stop as a pretext to accomplish some other purpose unrelated to the arrest or stop so long as the arrest or stop has a lawful basis. The main text gives the example of a drug investigator conducting a traffic stop on the basis of an observed traffic violation not because of concern with the traffic violation but because the investigator wishes to conduct a drug investigation during the course of the stop. The discussion in the main text continues to accurately reflect the law of pretextual stops generally, but the United States Supreme Court's decision in

---

27. *Id.* at ___, 813 S.E.2d at 844.

28. 583 U.S. ___, 138 S. Ct. 577 (2018).

29. *Id.* at 589.

30. 517 U.S. 806 (1996).

*Rodriguez v. United States*[31] significantly limits the scope of investigative activities unrelated to the legal basis for a stop that an officer may undertake. Thus, *Rodriguez* affects pretextual stops as a practical matter. *Rodriguez* is discussed in more detail on page 48 of the main text, below in this supplement, and in a new School of Government publication dealing specifically with North Carolina traffic stops.[32]

## Special Aspects of Stopping Authority (page 46)
### Investigative Stop Based on Reasonable Suspicion (page 46)
#### *Length of Time Allowed for an Investigative Stop* (page 46)
##### Officer's interaction with suspect after investigative stop is completed (page 47)

In *State v. Reed*,[33] the North Carolina Court of Appeals held over a dissent that the trial court erred by failing to suppress evidence seized pursuant to a consent search where the defendant was unlawfully seized at the time he gave consent to search. Though the stopping officer had issued the defendant a warning ticket, returned his license and paperwork, and told the defendant he was "completely done with the traffic stop,"[34] the officer nevertheless told the defendant to stay in his patrol car and another trooper was positioned outside the vehicle door. Under these circumstances, the court said, "[a] reasonable person in Defendant's position would not believe he was permitted to leave"[35] and the trial court should have suppressed evidence gathered pursuant to the consent search.[36] At the time of this writing, the North Carolina Supreme Court has issued a temporary stay in this case, so further review is possible.

##### United States Supreme Court case on delay after completed traffic stop (page 48)

This section of the main text discusses the United States Supreme Court decision in *Rodriguez v. United States*,[37] where the Court held that a "stop exceeding the time needed to handle the matter for which the stop was made violates the Constitution's shield against unreasonable seizures." The North Carolina appellate courts have applied *Rodriguez* or otherwise analyzed cases dealing with the length of time allowed for an investigative stop on several occasions subsequent to the publication of the main text.[38] In *State v. Bullock*,[39] an officer with experience on his department's drug interdiction team pulled the defendant over after observing him speeding, following a truck too closely, and weaving over the white line marking the edge of the road. In the course of the stop, the officer asked the defendant to exit his car and sit in the officer's patrol car, telling him that he would be receiving a warning rather than a ticket. Noting that an officer may order a driver of a lawfully stopped car to exit his vehicle as a matter of course,[40] the North Carolina Supreme Court determined that any amount of time added to the stop by asking the defendant to exit his car "was simply time spent pursuing the mission of the stop."[41] The officer also frisked the defendant for weapons before the defendant entered the officer's patrol

---

31. 575 U.S. ___, 135 S. Ct. 1609 (2015).

32. Shea Riggsbee Denning, Christopher Tyner & Jeff Welty, *Pulled Over: The Law of Traffic Stops and Offenses in North Carolina* 60–61 (UNC School of Government, 2017).

33. ___ N.C. App. ___, 810 S.E.2d 245, *temp. stay allowed*, ___ N.C. ___, 809 S.E.2d 130 (2018).

34. *Id.* at ___, 810 S.E.2d at 248.

35. *Id.* at ___, 810 S.E.2d at 249.

36. For a discussion of *Reed*, see Shea Denning, *Court of Appeals Reconsiders* State v. Reed *and Again Finds a Fourth Amendment Violation*, UNC Sch. of Gov't: N.C. Crim. L. Blog (Jan. 17, 2018), https://nccriminallaw.sog.unc.edu/court-appeals-reconsiders-state-v-reed-finds-fourth-amendment-violation.

37. 575 U.S. ___, ___, 135 S. Ct. 1609, 1612 (2015).

38. In addition to the discussion here, see the appendix for other North Carolina appellate cases on this issue as well as Shea Riggsbee Denning, Christopher Tyner & Jeff Welty, *Pulled Over: The Law of Traffic Stops and Offenses in North Carolina* 60–61 (UNC School of Government, 2017).

39. 370 N.C. 256 (2017).

40. The main text discusses this general rule on page 49.

41. *Bullock*, 370 N.C. at 261–62.

car. The court ruled that this frisk did not unconstitutionally prolong the stop for two independent reasons. First, the frisk enhanced the officer's safety and, the court said, "time devoted to officer safety is time that is reasonably required to complete" the mission of the stop.[42] As a second basis for the constitutionality of the frisk, the court determined that the eight or nine seconds required for the frisk did not measurably extend the duration of the stop. The court also determined that the officer's questioning of the defendant during the time required to run database checks related to the mission of the stop did not unlawfully extend the stop because the checks had to be run before the stop could be finished.[43] The court stated the rule of *Rodriguez* as follows: "Under *Rodriguez*, the duration of a traffic stop must be limited to the length of time that is reasonably necessary to accomplish the mission of the stop, unless reasonable suspicion of another crime arose before that mission was completed."[44] The court went on to explain that the "reasonable duration of a traffic stop . . . includes more than just the time needed to write a ticket" and that ordinary inquiries incident to the stop are part of an officer's mission.[45] The court identified driver's license and warrant checks as well as registration and insurance checks as among such ordinary inquiries.[46] The court also added that precautions related to officer safety, including criminal history checks, are within the mission of a traffic stop.[47] Finally, the court noted that investigations into unrelated crimes, even absent reasonable suspicion, are permitted if those investigations do not extend the duration of the stop.[48]

In *State v. Campola*,[49] the North Carolina Court of Appeals reiterated many of the points made by the state supreme court in *Bullock*. Consistent with *Rodriguez* and *Bullock*, the court stated that "database searches of driver's licenses, warrants, vehicle registrations, and proof of insurance all fall within the mission of a traffic stop" and also explained that criminal history checks were permissible officer safety precautions within the mission of the stop.[50] The court said that the stopping officer's request for backup, made because there were two occupants in the vehicle, also was a permissible safety precaution.[51]

### Footnote 201 (page 48)

The main text associated with footnote 201 explains that *Rodriguez* does not alter the general rule that an officer may lawfully extend a completed traffic stop if the officer develops reasonable suspicion of other criminal activity while otherwise diligently pursuing the mission of the stop, and the footnote itself provides examples of post-*Rodriguez* North Carolina appellate cases to that effect. Additional cases for this footnote include: *State v. Downey*, 370 N.C. 507 (2018) (reasonable suspicion supported extension of stop); *State v. Bullock*, 370 N.C. 256 (2017) (same); *State v. Sutton*, ___ N.C. App. ___, ___ S.E.2d ___, 2018 WL 2625844 (June 5, 2018) (same); *State v. Cox*, ___ N.C. App. ___, ___ S.E.2d ___, 2018 WL 2207337 (May 15, 2018) (same); *State v. Campola*, ___ N.C. App. ___, 812 S.E.2d 681 (2018) (same).

### Scope of Investigative Stop: Investigative Techniques (page 49)

#### Ordering driver and passengers out of vehicle (page 49)

The main text explains that the United States Supreme Court has ruled that an officer who has lawfully stopped a vehicle may order the driver and passengers out of the vehicle without showing any reason to do so under

---

42. *Id.* at 262.

43. For a case following the holding of *Bullock* that requiring a driver to exit his vehicle, frisking him, and making him sit in a patrol car while running records checks and being questioned did not unlawfully extend a stop, see *State v. Reed*, ___ N.C. App. ___, 810 S.E.2d 245, *temp. stay allowed*, ___ N.C. ___, 809 S.E.2d 130 (2018).

44. *Bullock*, 370 N.C. at 257.

45. *Id.*

46. *Id.*

47. *Id.*

48. *Id.*

49. ___ N.C. App. ___, 812 S.E.2d 681 (2018).

50. *Id.* at ___, 812 S.E.2d at 687–88.

51. *Id.*

the Fourth Amendment. The North Carolina Supreme Court explicitly recognized an officer's continued authority to do so in *State v. Bullock*.[52]

### Checking Division of Criminal Information or other information source (page 51)

The main text explains that after stopping a suspect, an officer may check for outstanding warrants and other criminally related information if the check does not unduly prolong the stop. In the context of lawful traffic stops, the North Carolina Supreme Court stated that it appeared, based on a decision of the United States Supreme Court, that conducting a criminal history check is an appropriate officer safety precaution inherent in the mission of a traffic stop.[53] Thus, in the context of traffic stops, it appears that the court would not consider the time necessary for such a check to constitute unduly prolonging the stop.

## The Arrest Warrant and Other Criminal Process (page 56)

Legislation enacted in 2017[54] amended G.S. 15A-304 in a manner bearing upon the discussion in the main text of arrest warrants and criminal summonses. On page 60, the main text explains that a criminal summons should be used instead of an arrest warrant when it appears that the defendant will come to court as required without the need to arrest the defendant and set conditions of pretrial release. For a brief period of time subsequent to the publication of the main text, G.S. 15A-304(b) expressed a preference that a judicial official issue a criminal summons rather than an arrest warrant in even stronger terms than was the case when the main text was published, providing that an issuing official "shall issue a criminal summons instead of a warrant, unless the official finds that the accused should be taken into custody."[55] The amended statute provided a non-exclusive list of circumstances to be considered in determining whether the accused should be taken into custody.[56] Legislation enacted in 2018[57] repealed the amendment just described, returning the relevant portion of the statute to the form it was in when the main text was published.

The same 2017 legislation placed new restrictions on citizen-initiated criminal process, one of which was eliminated by the 2018 legislation described above. Under the statute as amended in 2017, probable cause supporting citizen-initiated criminal process could only be provided by written affidavit. This change in the law affected the discussion in the "Issuance and content" section on pages 57 and 58 of the main text, which explains that a person may present facts supporting probable cause to a magistrate by either written affidavit or oral testimony. While the 2017 amendments were in effect, the discussion in the main text continued to be accurate where the person providing facts supporting probable cause was a sworn law enforcement officer. Under the 2018 legislation, effective October 1, 2018, citizen-initiated criminal process once again may be based on oral testimony, as was the case when the main text was published.

One of the changes to G.S. 15A-304 introduced by the 2017 legislation was not affected by the 2018 legislation. The statute now provides that in cases where the person providing probable cause information is not a sworn law enforcement officer, an issuing official "shall not issue a warrant for arrest and instead shall issue a criminal summons" unless: (1) there is corroborating testimony of the facts establishing probable cause from a sworn law enforcement officer or at least one disinterested witness, (2) the issuing official finds that obtaining investigation of the alleged offense by a law enforcement agency would constitute a substantial burden for

---

52. 370 N.C. 256 (2017) (driver).
53. *Id.*
54. S.L. 2017-176.
55. *Id.*
56. *Id.*
57. S.L. 2018-40.

the complainant, or (3) the issuing official finds substantial evidence of one or more grounds for taking the accused into custody as listed in G.S. 15A-304(b)(1).[58]

## Arrest Without a Warrant or Order for Arrest (page 62)
### Taking Custody of Juveniles for Delinquent Acts and Other Matters (page 66)

This section of the main text discusses the authority of law enforcement officers to take custody of juveniles under the age of 16 where there is probable cause to believe that the juvenile is delinquent and the same reasons exist to justify temporary custody as would justify a warrantless arrest of an adult. The Juvenile Justice Reinvestment Act, commonly known as the "raise the age" law, takes effect on December 1, 2019, and raises the age of juvenile jurisdiction to 18 for most purposes.[59] As it relates to this section of the main text, the raise the age law amends the definition of the term *delinquent juvenile* in G.S. 7B-1501(7) to include "[a]ny juvenile who, while less than 18 years of age but at least 16 years of age, commits a crime or an infraction under state law or under an ordinance of local government, excluding violation of the motor vehicle laws, or who commits indirect contempt by a juvenile as defined in G.S. 5A-31." Thus, after the raise the age law takes effect, the discussion in the main text regarding taking temporary custody of juveniles under the age of 16 also will be applicable to 16- and 17-year-olds, except where the offense at issue involves a violation of the motor vehicle laws.

## The Arrest Procedure (page 67)
### Entering Defendant's Home or Other Place of Residence without Consent or Exigent Circumstances (page 71)
#### *Exigent Circumstances That Justify Entering Premises* (page 74)

In *State v. Adams*,[60] the North Carolina Court of Appeals held that exigent circumstances supported officers entering the defendant's home to arrest him for resisting a public officer. While on routine patrol, officers observed the defendant driving a motor vehicle and developed reasonable suspicion that the defendant was driving while his license was revoked. The officers pulled into the defendant's driveway, where he had just parked, and initiated a traffic stop by activating blue lights. By the time the lights were activated, the defendant already had exited his vehicle and was walking towards the front door. An officer instructed the defendant to stop, but he disregarded the command, entered the front door, and attempted to close the door on an officer in pursuit. The officers prevented the defendant from closing the door, entered his home, and arrested him. The court found that the defendant's failure to stop for the blue lights and his disregard of the officer's commands gave the officers probable cause to arrest him for resisting an officer; the situation became one of "hot pursuit" as the defendant hurried toward the door to his house. Citing *United States v. Santana*,[61] the court of appeals held that the officers' hot pursuit of defendant was an exigent circumstance sufficient to justify a warrantless entry and arrest of the defendant inside his home.[62] The court rejected the defendant's argument that the entry was unreasonable because there was no threat of violence, no evidence subject to destruction, and no likelihood of the defendant fleeing his home to elude detection. The court also rejected the defendant's argument that the officers' decision to engage in hot pursuit was unreasonable.

---

58. *Id.*
59. *See generally* S.L. 2017-57, § 16D.4.
60. ___ N.C. App. ___, 794 S.E.2d 357 (2016).
61. 427 U.S. 38 (1976).
62. *Adams*, ___ N.C. App. at ___, 794 S.E.2d at 362–63.

## Completion of Custody of the Arrestee (page 79)
### Taking Fingerprints and Photographs (page 81)

This section of the main text divides its discussion of taking fingerprints and photographs of arrestees into separate sections, one dealing with adults and one dealing with juveniles. Footnote 427 explains that the term "adult" is not used in the statutes but is used in the main text to refer to (1) a person who commits a criminal offense on or after his or her 16th birthday; (2) a juvenile who commits a criminal offense and is emancipated, married, or in the armed services; or (3) a juvenile who commits a criminal offense and has been previously convicted of an offense in superior court. The footnote cites G.S. 7B-1604, a statute describing limitations on juvenile court jurisdiction, as the basis for the delineation made in the main text between adults and juveniles. The Juvenile Justice Reinvestment Act, commonly known as the "raise the age" law, takes effect on December 1, 2019, and, generally speaking, raises the age of juvenile jurisdiction to 18 for most purposes. The law amends G.S. 7B-1604 in a manner that affects two of the categories of "adult[s]" outlined in the footnote. First, it provides a general rule that a juvenile is subject to prosecution as an adult upon reaching age 18, rather than age 16. Second, the law amends G.S. 7B-1604 to provide that a juvenile who has previously been convicted in either district or superior court for a felony or a misdemeanor, including a violation of the motor vehicle laws under state law, shall be prosecuted as an adult for any criminal offense committed subsequent to that conviction. The main text goes on to say, on page 82, that there is "some uncertainty about what age constitutes an adult for the purpose of fingerprinting and photographing" but explains that the more persuasive view is that an adult is a person 16 years old or older. The basis for that view being the persuasive one is laid out in footnote 439, and is grounded in a detailed analysis of legislative history and case law, as well as a careful parsing of statutory language, including portions of Article 15 of Chapter 7B affected by the raise the age law. A portion of the analysis in footnote 439 says that because a particular subsection of G.S. 15A-502, the statute governing the photographing and fingerprinting of persons charged with criminal offenses, generally prohibits the taking of photographs or fingerprints "of a juvenile alleged to be delinquent," the better reading of the statute as a whole is that 16- and 17-year-olds are subject to being fingerprinted and photographed because, under current law, only a juvenile under 16 years of age may be alleged to be delinquent. As noted, when the raise the age law becomes effective, many 16- and 17-year-olds who would have been charged with criminal offenses as adults under current law instead will be alleged to be delinquent. This section of the main text will be revised when it becomes clearer how the raise the age law will affect fingerprinting and photographing of arrestees under the age of 18, but as the effective date of the raise the age law draws nearer, the advice in the final sentence of the section entitled "Adults" in the main text is increasingly valuable: Officers may wish to consult their agency's legal advisor or their district attorney to determine how to handle fingerprinting and photographing 16- and 17-year-olds.

### Considering Pretrial Release Conditions (page 86)

In *State v. Mitchell*,[63] the North Carolina Court of Appeals held that judicially ordered restrictions prohibiting the defendant from contacting his romantic partner, who was the alleged victim of the defendant's assaultive conduct, were in effect while the defendant was in pretrial detention despite the fact that the restrictions were described in portions of court orders ostensibly setting the defendant's conditions of pretrial release. In reaching this holding, the court rejected the defendant's argument that he did not become subject to the restrictions until he was released from detention and, thus, that he did not violate the restrictions by contacting his romantic partner while detained. The court reasoned that the relevant court orders were in effect and prohibited the defendant's conduct regardless of the fact that he had not been released from detention.

---

63. ___ N.C. App. ___, ___ S.E.2d. ___, 2018 WL 2630594 (June 5, 2018).

# Chapter 2 Appendix: Case Summaries

## Arrests, Investigative Stops, and Related Issues (page 97)

### The Authority to Make an Investigative Stop: Reasonable Suspicion (page 99)
**Determination of Reasonable Suspicion** (page 99)
*Generally* (page 99)
**NORTH CAROLINA SUPREME COURT** (page 102)

*State v. Nicholson*, ___ N.C. ___, 813 S.E.2d 840 (2018). On appeal from the decision of a divided panel of the court of appeals, ___ N.C. App. ___, 805 S.E.2d 348 (2017), the court reversed, holding that an officer's decision to briefly detain the defendant for questioning was supported by reasonable suspicion of criminal activity. While on patrol at 4 a.m., Lieutenant Marotz noticed a car parked in a turn lane of the street, with its headlights on but no turn signal blinking. Marotz saw two men inside the vehicle, one in the driver's seat and the other—later identified as the defendant—in the seat directly behind the driver. The windows were down despite rain and low temperatures. As Marotz pulled alongside the vehicle, he saw the defendant pull down a hood or toboggan-style mask with holes for the eyes, but then push the item back up when he saw the officer. Marotz asked the two whether everything was okay and they responded that it was. The driver said that the man in the back was his brother and they had been arguing. The driver said the argument was over and everything was okay. Sensing that something was not right, the officer again asked if they were okay, and they nodded that they were. Then the driver moved his hand near his neck, "scratching or doing something with his hand." Still feeling that something was amiss, Marotz drove to a nearby gas station to observe the situation. After the car remained immobile in the turn lane for another half minute, Marotz got out of his vehicle and started on foot towards the car. The defendant stepped out of the vehicle and the driver began to edge the car forward. Marotz asked the driver what he was doing and the driver said he was late and had to get to work. The officer again asked whether everything was okay and the men said that everything was fine. However, although the driver responded "yes" to the officer's question, he shook his head "no." This prompted the officer to further question the defendant. The driver insisted he just had to get to work and the officer told him to go. After the driver left, the defendant asked the officer if he could walk to a nearby store. The officer responded, "[H]ang tight for me just a second . . . you don't have any weapons on you, do you?" The defendant said he had a knife but a frisk by a backup officer did not reveal a weapon. After additional questioning the officers learned the defendant's identity and told him he was free to go. Later that day the driver reported to the police that the defendant was not his brother and had been robbing him when Marotz pulled up. The defendant held a knife to the driver's throat and demanded money. Officers later found a steak knife in the back seat of the vehicle. The defendant was charged with armed robbery and he moved to suppress the evidence obtained as a result of his seizure by Marotz. The parties agreed that the defendant was seized when Marotz told him to "hang tight." The court found that the circumstances established a reasonable, articulable suspicion that criminal activity was afoot. Although the facts might not establish reasonable suspicion when viewed in isolation, when considered in their totality they could lead a reasonable officer to suspect that he had just happened upon a robbery in progress. The court also found that the court of appeals placed undue weight on Marotz's subjective interpretation of the facts (the officer's testimony suggested that he did not believe he had reasonable suspicion of criminal activity), rather than focusing on how an objective, reasonable officer would have viewed them. The court noted that an action is reasonable under the Fourth Amendment regardless of the officer's state of mind, if the circumstances viewed objectively justify the action. Here they do.

*State v. Goins*, 370 N.C. 157 (2017). For the reasons stated in the dissenting opinion below, the court reversed the decision of the court of appeals in *State v. Goins*, ___ N.C. App. ___, 789 S.E.2d 466 (2016). In that case, the court of appeals held, over a dissent, that a stop of the defendant's vehicle was not supported by reasonable suspicion. Just after midnight, officers were on patrol near an apartment complex that they knew as an area of high crime and drug activity. The officers observed a car, a Hyundai Elantra, enter the apartment complex parking lot and drive toward a man standing in front of one of the apartment buildings. The man looked directly at their patrol vehicle and then made a loud "warning noise" directed at the Elantra. Immediately thereafter, the Elantra accelerated and quickly exited the apartment complex, an action the trial court characterized as unprovoked fleeing from the officers. The dissenting judge in the court of appeals concluded, under a totality of the circumstances analysis, that the officers had reasonable suspicion to justify an investigatory stop of the Elantra based on the vehicle's presence in a high-crime area and its apparent flight from the officers.

## NORTH CAROLINA COURT OF APPEALS (page 106)

*State v. Sutton*, ___ N.C. App. ___, S.E.2d ___, 2018 WL 2625844 (June 5, 2018). In this drug trafficking case, the court held that the fact that the defendant's truck crossed over a double yellow line justified the stop. The officer saw the defendant's vehicle cross the center line of the road by about 1 inch. The court stated:

> [T]here is a "bright line" rule in some traffic stop cases. Here, the bright line is a double yellow line down the center of the road. Where a vehicle actually crosses over the double yellow lines in the center of a road, even once, and even without endangering any other drivers, the driver has committed a traffic violation of N.C. Gen. Stat. § 20-146 (2017). This is a "readily observable" traffic violation and the officer may stop the driver without violating his constitutional rights.

*State v. Walker*, ___ N.C. App. ___, 806 S.E.2d 326 (2017). The court ruled that reasonable suspicion did not exist to support a stop. At approximately 5 p.m., dispatch notified a trooper on routine patrol that an informant–driver reported that another driver was driving while intoxicated. The informant reported that the driver was driving from the Hubert area toward Jacksonville, traveling about 80 to 100 m.p.h. while drinking a beer. He also claimed that the driver was driving "very erratically" and almost ran him off the road "a few times." While the trooper was responding to the dispatch, the informant flagged him down and said that the vehicle in question had just passed through the intersection on U.S. 258, heading toward Richlands. The trooper headed in that direction and stopped the defendant's vehicle within 1/10 of a mile of the intersection. The defendant was arrested and charged with DWI and careless and reckless driving. The defendant unsuccessfully moved to suppress in district court and appealed to superior court. After a hearing, the superior court granted the motion to suppress. The court of appeals found that the tip did not have sufficient indicia of reliability to provide reasonable suspicion for the stop. Although the informant was not anonymous, the informant was unable to specifically point out the defendant's vehicle to the trooper because the vehicle was out of sight. The trooper did not observe the vehicle being driven in a suspicious or erratic fashion. Additionally, it is unknown whether the trooper had the vehicle's license plate number before or after the stop and whether the trooper had any vehicle description besides a "gray Ford passenger vehicle." The court distinguished prior case law involving tips that provided enough information so that there was no doubt as to which particular vehicle was being reported. Here, the informant's ambiguous description did not specify a particular vehicle. Additionally, no other circumstances enabled the trooper to further corroborate the tip; the trooper did not witness the vehicle behaving as described by the informant.

*State v. Sauls*, ___ N.C. App. ___, 807 S.E.2d 155 (2017). The court ruled that reasonable suspicion supported the traffic stop. At the time of the stop it was very late at night, the defendant's vehicle was idling in front of a closed business, the business and surrounding properties had experienced several break-ins, and the defendant pulled away when the officer approached the car. Considered together, these facts provided an objective justification for stopping the defendant.

**State v. Evans**, ___ N.C. App. ___, 795 S.E.2d 444 (2017). The court ruled that reasonable suspicion supported the stop. An officer patrolling a "known drug corridor" at 4 a.m. observed the defendant's car stopped in the lane of traffic. An unidentified pedestrian approached the defendant's car and leaned in the window. The officer found these actions to be indicative of a drug transaction and thus conducted the stop.

**State v. Watson**, ___ N.C. App. ___, 792 S.E.2d 873 (2016). In this drug case, the trial court erred by denying the defendant's motion to suppress drug evidence seized after a traffic stop where the officer had no reasonable suspicion to stop the defendant's vehicle. Officers received a tip from a confidential informant regarding "suspicious" packages that the defendant had received from a local UPS store. The informant was an employee of the UPS store trained to detect narcotics; the informant had successfully notified the police about packages later found to contain illegal drugs and these tips were used to secure a number of felony drug convictions. With respect to the incident in question, the informant advised the police that a man, later identified as the defendant, had arrived at the UPS store in a truck and retrieved packages with a Utah return address when in fact the packages had been sent from Arizona. After receiving this tip, the police arrived at the store, observed the defendant driving away, and initiated a traffic stop. During the stop they conducted a canine sniff, which led to the discovery of drugs inside the packages. Holding that the motion to suppress should have been granted, the court noted that there is nothing illegal about receiving a package with a return address that differs from the actual shipping address; in fact there are number of innocent explanations for why this could have occurred. Although innocent factors, when considered together, may give rise to reasonable suspicion, the court noted that it was unable to find any case where reasonable suspicion was based solely on a suspicious return address. Here, the trial court made no finding that the informant or the police had any prior experience with the defendant; that the origination city was known as a drug source locale; nor that the packages were sealed suspiciously, had a suspicious weight based on their size, had handwritten labels, or had a suspicious odor.

### DWI Stops (page 120)
**NORTH CAROLINA COURT OF APPEALS** (page 122)

**State v. Mangum**, ___ N.C. App. ___, 795 S.E.2d 106 (2016). The court ruled that a vehicle stop was supported by reasonable suspicion. An officer received an anonymous report that a drunk driver was operating a black, four-door Hyundai headed north on Highland Capital Boulevard. The officer located the vehicle as reported and observed that the defendant drove roughly 15 m.p.h. below the 35 m.p.h. speed limit; that the defendant stopped at an intersection without a stop sign or traffic signal for "longer than usual"; that the defendant stopped at a railroad crossing and remained motionless for 15 to 20 seconds, although no train was coming and there was no signal to stop; that after the officer activated his blue lights, the defendant continued driving for approximately two minutes, eventually stopping in the middle of the road, and in a portion of the road with no bank or curb, having passed several safe places to pull over.

### Non-DWI Traffic Stops (page 125)
**NORTH CAROLINA SUPREME COURT** (page 126)

**State v. Johnson**, 370 N.C. 32 (2017). The supreme court reversed the decision below, ___ N.C. App. ___, 784 S.E.2d 633 (2016), a case summarized on page 129 of the main text, which had held that because a police officer lacked reasonable suspicion for a traffic stop in this DWI case, the trial court erred by denying the defendant's motion to suppress. The defendant was stopped at a red light on a snowy evening. When the light turned green, the officer saw the defendant's truck abruptly accelerate, turn sharply left, and fishtail. The officer pulled the defendant over for driving at an unsafe speed given the road conditions. The supreme court held that the officer had reasonable suspicion to stop the defendant's vehicle. It noted that G.S. 20-141(a) provides that "[n]o person shall drive a vehicle on a highway or in a public vehicular area at a speed greater than is reasonable and prudent under the conditions then existing." The court concluded:

> All of these facts show that it was reasonable for [the] Officer . . . to believe that defendant's truck had fishtailed, and that defendant had lost control of his truck, because of defendant's abrupt acceleration while turning in the snow. It is common knowledge that drivers must drive more slowly when it is snowing, because it is easier to lose control of a vehicle on snowy roads than on clear ones. And any time that a driver loses control of his vehicle, he is in danger of damaging that vehicle or other vehicles, and of injuring himself or others. So, under the totality of these circumstances, it was reasonable for [the] Officer . . . to believe that defendant had violated [G.S.] 20-141(a) by driving too quickly given the conditions of the road.

The court further noted that no actual traffic violation need have occurred for a stop to be initiated. It clarified: "To meet the reasonable suspicion standard, it is enough for the officer to reasonably believe that a driver has violated the law."

### NORTH CAROLINA COURT OF APPEALS (page 129)

**State v. Jones**, ___ N.C. App. ___, 813 S.E.2d 668 (2018). An officer's observation of a single instance of a vehicle crossing the double yellow centerline in violation of state motor vehicle law provided reasonable suspicion to support the traffic stop. While traveling southbound on Highway 32, N.C. Highway Patrol Trooper Myers was notified by dispatch that a caller had reported a black Chevrolet truck traveling northbound on Highway 32 at a careless, reckless, and high speed. Myers then saw a black Chevrolet truck traveling northbound cross the center double yellow line. Myers initiated a traffic stop, which resulted in impaired driving charges. The defendant argued that the stop was not supported by reasonable suspicion because Myers did not corroborate the caller's information. The court rejected this argument, noting that Myers's own observation of the vehicle driving left of center provided reasonable suspicion for the stop. Under G.S. 20-150(d), crossing a double yellow centerline constitutes a traffic violation. Citing prior case law, the court stated that an officer's observation of such a violation is sufficient to constitute reasonable suspicion for a traffic stop.

**State v. Eldridge**, ___ N.C. App. ___, 790 S.E.2d 740 (2016). The court ruled that the trial court erred by denying the defendant's motion to suppress where a stop was based on an officer's mistake of law that was not objectively reasonable. An officer stopped a vehicle registered in Tennessee for driving without an exterior mirror on the driver's side of the vehicle. The officer was not aware that the relevant statute—G.S. 20-126(b)—does not apply to vehicles registered out-of-state. A subsequent consent search led to the discovery of controlled substances and drug charges. On appeal, the State conceded, and the court concluded, following *Heien v. North Carolina*, 135 S. Ct. 530 (2014), that the officer's mistake of law was not reasonable. Looking for guidance in other jurisdictions that have interpreted *Heien*, the court noted that cases from other jurisdictions "establish that in order for an officer's mistake of law while enforcing a statute to be objectively reasonable, the statute at issue must be ambiguous." "Moreover," the court noted, "some courts applying *Heien* have further required that there be an absence of settled case law interpreting the statute at issue in order for the officer's mistake of law to be deemed objectively reasonable." The court concluded that the statute at issue was clear and unambiguous; as a result, "a reasonable officer reading this statute would understand the requirement that a vehicle be equipped with a driver's side exterior mirror does not apply to vehicles that—like Defendant's vehicle—are registered in another state."

## Special Aspects of Stopping Authority (page 137)
*Length of Time Allowed for an Investigative Stop* (page 137)
NORTH CAROLINA SUPREME COURT (page 139)

**State v. Downey**, 370 N.C. 507 (2018). The court per curiam affirmed a divided decision of the court of appeals, ___ N.C. App. ___, 796 S.E.2d 517 (2017), upholding an order denying the defendant's motion to suppress. Over a dissent, the court of appeals had held that reasonable suspicion supported extension of a traffic stop. After an officer stopped the defendant for a traffic violation, he approached the vehicle and asked to see the defendant's driver's license and registration. As the defendant complied, the officer noticed that his hands were shaking, his breathing was rapid, and he failed to make eye contact. He also noticed a prepaid cell phone inside the vehicle and a Black Ice air freshener. The officer had learned during drug interdiction training that Black Ice freshener is frequently used by drug traffickers because of its strong scent and that prepaid cell phones are commonly used in drug trafficking. The officer determined that the car was not registered to the defendant, and he knew from his training that third-party vehicles are often used by drug traffickers. In response to questioning about why the defendant was in the area, the defendant provided vague answers. When the officer asked the defendant about his criminal history, the defendant responded that he had served time for breaking and entering and that he had a cocaine-related drug conviction. After issuing the defendant a warning ticket for the traffic violation and returning his documentation, the officer continued to question the defendant and asked for consent to search the vehicle. The defendant declined. He also declined consent to a canine sniff. The officer then called for a canine unit, which arrived 14 minutes after the initial stop ended. An alert led to a search of the vehicle and the discovery of contraband. The court of appeals rejected the defendant's argument that the officer lacked reasonable suspicion to extend the traffic stop, noting that before and during the time in which the officer prepared the warning citation, he observed the defendant's nervous behavior, he noted use of a particular brand of powerful air freshener favored by drug traffickers, he noticed the defendant's prepaid cell phone, he learned that the defendant's car was registered to someone else and that the defendant had a prior conviction for a drug offense, and the defendant provided only vague and suspicious answers to the officer's questions about why he was in the area. These circumstances, the court of appeals held, constituted reasonable suspicion to extend the duration of the stop.

**State v. Bullock**, 370 N.C. 256 (2017). On an appeal from a divided panel of the court of appeals, ___ N.C. App. ___, 785 S.E.2d 746 (2016), the court reversed, concluding that the stop at issue, which was initiated based on traffic violations and where heroin ultimately was discovered, was not unduly prolonged under *Rodriguez*, 575 U.S. ___, 135 S. Ct. 1609 (2017). The trial court denied the defendant's motion to suppress and the court of appeals reversed, concluding that the stop had been unduly prolonged. During the stop, the defendant's hand trembled as he provided his license to the stopping officer. Although the car was a rental vehicle, the defendant was not listed as a driver on the rental agreement. The officer noticed that the defendant had two cell phones, a fact he associated, based on experience, with transporting drugs. The defendant was stopped on I-85, a major drug trafficking thoroughfare. When the officer asked the defendant where he was going, the defendant said he was going to his girlfriend's house on Century Oaks Drive and that he had missed his exit. The officer knew, however, that the defendant was well past the exit for that location, having passed three exits that would have taken him there. The defendant said he had recently moved to North Carolina. The officer asked the defendant to step out of the vehicle and sit in the patrol car, telling him that he would receive a warning, not a ticket. At this point the officer frisked the defendant, finding $372 in cash. The defendant sat in the patrol car while the officer ran the defendant's information through law enforcement databases, and the two continued to talk. The defendant gave contradictory statements about his girlfriend. Although the defendant made eye contact with the officer when answering certain questions, he looked away when asked about his girlfriend and where he was traveling. The database checks revealed that the defendant was issued a driver's license in 2000 and that he had a criminal history in North Carolina starting in 2001, facts contradicting his earlier claim to have just moved to the state. The officer asked the defendant for permission to search the vehicle. The defendant agreed to let the officer search the vehicle but declined to allow a search of a bag and two hoodies. When the officer found the bag and hoodies in the trunk, the defendant quickly objected that the bag was not his, contradicting an earlier statement, and said he did not want it searched. The officer put the bag on the ground and a police dog alerted to it. Officers opened the bag and found a large amount of heroin. The defendant did not challenge the validity of the initial stop. The court began by noting that during a lawful stop, an officer can ask the driver to exit the vehicle. Next, it held that the frisk was lawful for two reasons. First, frisking the defendant before putting him in the patrol car enhanced officer safety. And second, where, as here, the frisk lasted only eight to nine seconds, it did not measurably prolong the stop so as to require reasonable suspicion. The court went on to find that asking the defendant to sit in the patrol car did not unlawfully extend the stop. The officer was required to check three databases before the stop could be finished and it was not prolonged by having the defendant in the patrol car while this was done. This action took a few minutes to complete and while it was being done, the officer was free to talk with the defendant "at least up until the moment that all three database checks had been completed." The court went on to conclude that the conversation the two had while the database checks were running provided reasonable suspicion to prolong the stop. It noted that I-85 is a major drug trafficking corridor, the defendant was nervous and had two cell phones, the rental car was in someone else's name, the defendant gave an illogical account of where he was going, and cash was discovered during the frisk. All of these facts provided reasonable suspicion of drug activity that justified prolonging the stop shortly after the defendant entered the patrol car. There, as he continued his conversation with the officer, he gave inconsistent statements about his girlfriend and the database check revealed that he had not been truthful about a recent move to North Carolina. This, combined with the defendant's broken eye contact, allowed the officer to extend the stop for purposes of the dog sniff.

### NORTH CAROLINA COURT OF APPEALS (page 140)

**State v. Sutton**, ___ N.C. App. ___, ___ S.E.2d ___, 2018 WL 2625844 (June 5, 2018). The court ruled that after a proper traffic stop, an officer had reasonable suspicion to extend the stop for six or seven minutes for a dog sniff. The officer was patrolling a road because of complaints about drug activity and had been advised by the SBI to be on the lookout for the defendant based upon reports that he was bringing large quantities of methamphetamine to a supplier who lived off of the road. After the officer stopped the defendant's vehicle for an observed traffic violation, he identified the defendant as the person noted in the lookout warning. The defendant was confused, spoke so quickly that he was hard to understand, and began to stutter and mumble. The defendant did not make eye contact with the officer and his nervousness was "much more extreme" than a typical stopped driver. His eyes were bloodshot and glassy and the skin under his eyes was ashy. Based on his training and experience, the officer believed the defendant's behavior and appearance were consistent with methamphetamine use. The defendant told the officer he was going to "Rabbit's" house. The officer knew that "Rabbit" was involved with methamphetamine and lived nearby. When the defendant exited his car, he put his hand on the car for stability. These facts alone could have given the officer reasonable suspicion. But additionally, a woman the officer knew that had previously given drug information to law enforcement approached and told the officer she had talked to Rabbit and the defendant had "dope in the vehicle." These facts were more than sufficient to give the officer a reasonable suspicion that the defendant had drugs in his vehicle and justify extension of the stop for a dog sniff.

**State v. Cox,** ___ N.C. App. ___, ___ S.E.2d ___, 2018 WL 2207337 (May 15, 2018). The court ruled that the traffic stop at issue was not unduly extended. The defendant, a passenger in the stopped vehicle, argued that officers extended, without reasonable suspicion, the traffic stop after issuing the driver a warning citation. The stopping officer had extensive training in drug interdiction, including the detection of behaviors by individuals tending to indicate the use, transportation, and other activity associated with controlled substances, and had investigated more than 100 drug cases. The officer observed a sufficient number of "red flags" before issuing the warning citation to support a reasonable suspicion of criminal activity and therefore justify extending the stop. When the officer first encountered the vehicle, he observed body language by both the driver and the defendant that he considered evasive; the driver exhibited extreme and continued nervousness throughout the stop and was unable to produce any form of personal identification; the driver and the defendant gave conflicting accounts of their travel plans and their relationship to each other; the officer observed an open sore on the defendant's face that appeared, based on the officer's training and experience, related to the use of methamphetamine; and background checks revealed that the driver had an expired license.

**State v. Campola,** ___ N.C. App. ___, 812 S.E.2d 681 (2018). The court ruled that an officer had reasonable suspicion to prolong a traffic stop. A six-year officer who had received training in identification of drugs pulled into the parking lot of a Motel 6, a high-crime area. When he entered the lot, he saw two men sitting in a car. After the officer passed, the vehicle exited the lot at high speed. The officer stopped the car after observing a traffic violation. The vehicle displayed a temporary license tag. When the officer approached for the driver's information, the driver was "more nervous than usual." The officer asked why the two were at the motel, and the driver stated that they did not enter a room there. The passenger—the defendant—did not have any identifying documents but gave the officer his name. The officer went to his patrol car to enter the information in his computer and called for backup, as required by department regulations when more than one person is in a stopped vehicle. While waiting for backup to arrive, he entered the vehicle's VIN number in a 50-state database, not having a state registration to enter. He determined that the vehicle was not stolen. Although neither the driver nor the passenger had outstanding warrants, both had multiple prior drug arrests. Shortly after, and 12 minutes after the stop began, the backup officer arrived. The two approached the vehicle some 14 minutes after the stop was initiated. The stopping officer asked the driver to step to the rear of the vehicle so that they could see the intersection where the traffic violation occurred. The officer gave the driver a warning, returned his documents, and asked to search the vehicle. The driver declined. While the stopping officer was speaking with the driver, the backup officer approached the defendant and saw a syringe in the driver's seat. He asked the defendant to step out of the car and the defendant complied, at which point the officer saw a second syringe in the passenger seat. Four minutes into these conversations, the backup officer informed the stopping officer of the syringes. The stopping officer asked the driver if he was a diabetic and the driver said that he was not. The stopping officer then searched the vehicle, finding the contraband at issue. On appeal, the court held that the stop was not improperly extended. It noted that the stopping officer was engaged in "conduct within the scope of his mission" until the backup officer arrived after 12 minutes. Database searches of driver's licenses, warrants, vehicle registrations, and proof of insurance all fall within the mission of a traffic stop. Additionally the officer's research into the men's criminal histories was permitted as a precaution related to the traffic stop, as was the stopping officer's request for backup. Because officer safety stems from the mission of the traffic stop itself, time devoted to officer safety is time reasonably required to complete the mission of the stop. Even if a call for backup were not an appropriate safety precaution, here the backup call did not actually extend the stop because the stopping officer was still doing the required searches when the backup officer arrived. By the time the backup officer arrived, the stopping officer had developed a reasonable suspicion of criminal activity sufficient to extend the stop. The stopping officer was a trained officer who had participated in 100 drug arrests, he saw the driver and passenger in a high-crime area, after he drove by them they took off at a high speed and made an illegal turn, the driver informed the officer that the two were at the motel but did not go into a motel room, the driver was unusually nervous, and both men had multiple prior drug arrests. These facts provided reasonable suspicion to extend the stop. Even if these facts were insufficient, other facts support a conclusion that reasonable suspicion existed, including the men's surprise at seeing the officer in the motel lot, the titling of the vehicle to someone other than the driver or passenger, the driver's statement that he met a friend at the motel but did not know the friend's name, and the officer's recognition of the defendant as someone who had been involved in illegal drug activity. Finally, drawing on some of the same facts, the court rejected the defendant's argument that any reasonable suspicion supporting extension of the stop was not particularized to him. The court also noted that an officer may stop and detain a vehicle and its occupants if the officer has reasonable suspicion that criminal activity is afoot.

**State v. Bullock**, ___ N.C. App. ___, 811 S.E.2d 713 (2018). The court rejected the defendant's argument that his consent to search his rental vehicle was involuntary because it was given at a time when a traffic stop had been unduly prolonged. Specifically, the defendant argued that the stop was prolonged because of questioning by the officer and the time he was detained while waiting for a second officer to arrive to assist with the search. The case was before the court on remand from the state supreme court. That court had held that the initial traffic stop was valid, the officer lawfully frisked the defendant without prolonging the stop, the officer's database checks on the defendant's license did not unduly prolong the stop, and the conversation that occurred was sufficient to form reasonable suspicion authorizing the dog sniff of the vehicle and bag. Because all parts of the stop were lawfully extended, the trial court did not err in determining that the defendant's consent to search his vehicle was voluntary.

**State v. Reed,** ___ N.C. App. ___, 810 S.E.2d 245, *temp. stay allowed*, ___ N.C. ___, 809 S.E.2d 130 (2018). On remand from the North Carolina Supreme Court for consideration in light of *State v. Bullock*, 370 N.C. 256 (2017), the court held—over a dissent—that the trial court erred by denying the defendant's motion to suppress evidence obtained during a traffic stop. Finding itself bound by *Bullock*, the court concluded that the officer's actions requiring the defendant to exit his car, frisking him, and making him sit in the patrol car while the officer—Trooper Lamm—ran records checks and questioned the defendant, did not unlawfully extend the stop under *Rodriguez v. United States*, 575 U.S. ___, 135 S. Ct. 1609 (2017). However, the court went on to find that the case was distinguishable from *Bullock* because here, after the officer returned the defendant's paperwork and issued the warning ticket, the defendant remained unlawfully seized in the patrol car. The court explained:

> [A] reasonable person in Defendant's position would not believe he was permitted to leave. When Trooper Lamm returned Defendant's paperwork, Defendant was sitting in the patrol car. Trooper Lamm continued to question Defendant as he sat in the patrol car. When the trooper left the patrol car to seek [the passenger's] consent to search the rental car, he told Defendant to "sit tight." At this point, a second trooper was present on the scene, and stood directly beside the passenger door of Trooper Lamm's vehicle where Defendant sat. Moreover, at trial Trooper Lamm admitted at this point Defendant was not allowed to leave the patrol car.

Because a reasonable person in the defendant's position "would not feel free to leave when one trooper told him to stay in the patrol car, and another trooper was positioned outside the vehicle door," the defendant remained seized after his paperwork was returned. Thus, reasonable suspicion was required for the extension of the stop. Here, no such suspicion existed. Although the defendant appeared nervous; the passenger held a dog in her lap; dog food was scattered across the floorboard of the vehicle; and the car contained air fresheners, trash, and energy drinks, this was "legal activity consistent with lawful travel." And, while the officer initially had suspicions concerning the rental car agreement, he communicated with the rental company and confirmed everything was fine.

**State v. Parker,** ___ N.C. App. ___, 807 S.E.2d 617 (2017). Because the trial court's findings of fact did not support its conclusion that the defendant was legally seized at the time he consented to a search of his person, the court reversed the trial court's order denying the defendant's motion to suppress contraband found on his person. Officers were conducting surveillance on a known drug house. They noticed the defendant leave the residence in a truck and return 20 minutes later. He parked his truck in the driveway and walked toward a woman in the driveway of a nearby residence. The two began yelling at each other. Thinking the confrontation would escalate, the officers got out of their vehicle and separated the two. One officer asked the defendant for his identification. The officer checked the defendant's record, verifying that the defendant had no pending charges. Without returning the defendant's identification, the officer then asked the defendant if he had any narcotics on him and the defendant replied that he did not. At the officer's request, the defendant consented to a search of his person and vehicle. Drugs were found in his pants pocket. On appeal, the defendant argued that when the officer failed to return his identification after finding no outstanding warrants and after the initial reason for the detention was satisfied, the seizure became unlawful and the defendant's consent was not voluntary. The court agreed. It noted that the officer failed to return the defendant's identification before pursuing an inquiry into possession of drugs. It found that the trial court's order failed to provide findings of fact which would give rise to a reasonable suspicion that the defendant was otherwise subject to detention. Absent a reasonable suspicion to justify further delay, retaining the defendant's driver's license beyond the point of satisfying the initial purpose of the detention—de-escalating the conflict, checking the defendant's identification, and verifying that he had no outstanding warrants—was unreasonable. Thus, the defendant's consent to search his person, given during the period of unreasonable detention, was not voluntary.

**FEDERAL APPELLATE COURTS** (page 143)

*State v. White,* 836 F.3d 437 (2016). A local West Virginia law enforcement officer stopped a car that had veered out of its lane. In addition to the driver, there was a front seat passenger, the defendant, and one back seat passenger, Bone. When approaching the driver's window, the officer smelled an odor of burned marijuana emanating from the car. The driver, whom the officer concluded was not impaired, denied knowledge of the marijuana. The officer requested that the defendant exit the car and asked him about the marijuana odor, but he denied anything illegal in the car. While talking with Bone, the officer saw a firearm in a piece of plastic molding on the front side of the passenger seat where the defendant had been sitting. The defendant was arrested and later convicted in federal district court of possession of a firearm by a felon.

The defendant conceded that the stop of the vehicle was supported by reasonable suspicion of a traffic violation under West Virginia law, but he contended that the officer unconstitutionally prolonged the stop. The Fourth Circuit noted that its case law provides that the odor of marijuana alone can provide probable cause to believe marijuana is present in a particular place. Thus, the officer had reasonable suspicion to extend the traffic stop to investigate the marijuana odor, and during that investigation the officer found the firearm. The court ruled that therefore the officer did not unconstitutionally prolong the traffic stop.

### *Scope of an Investigative Stop* (page 143)

On page 146 of the main text, the first case summarized in this section from the North Carolina Court of Appeals, *State v. Johnson*, contains a citation error. The correct citation for the case summarized is: *State v. Johnson*, ___ N.C. App. ___, 783 S.E.2d 753 (2016).

### *Ordering People Out of a Vehicle after a Lawful Stop* (page 151)

**NORTH CAROLINA SUPREME COURT** (page 151)

*State v. Bullock,* 370 N.C. 256 (2017). The North Carolina Supreme Court reiterated that an officer may, as a matter of course, order a driver of a lawfully stopped vehicle to exit the vehicle.

## When an Officer's Interaction with a Person Is a Seizure under the Fourth Amendment (page 154)

**NORTH CAROLINA COURT OF APPEALS** (page 157)

*State v. Turnage,* ___ N.C. App. ___, ___ S.E.2d ___, 2018 WL 2207325 (May 15, 2018), *temp. stay allowed,* ___ N.C. ___, 814 S.E.2d 459 (June 20, 2018). Citing *Hodari D.*, the court noted that a show of authority by law enforcement does not rise to the level of a seizure unless the suspect submits to that authority or is physically restrained. Here, for unknown reasons the driver of a van and the defendant stopped the vehicle in the middle of the road before any show of authority from law enforcement. The detective's later activation of blue lights did not constitute a seizure because the defendant did not yield to the show of authority. The defendant was not seized until the vehicle was stopped during a subsequent chase. Criminal activity observed by the officer during the chase and his observation of the two minor children in the van justified the arrest for fleeing to elude, resisting an officer, and child abuse.

**State v. Burwell,** ___ N.C. App. ___, 808 S.E.2d 583 (2017). The court ruled that an arrest occurs when, under G.S. 122C-303, an officer takes a publicly intoxicated person to jail to assist that person and the action is taken against the person's will.

**State v. Wilson,** ___ N.C. App. ___, 793 S.E.2d 737 (2016), *aff'd per curiam*, 370 N.C. 389 (2017). In this impaired driving case, the court held, over a dissent, that the trial court properly denied the defendant's motion to suppress because no seizure occurred. An officer went to a residence to find a man who had outstanding warrants for his arrest. While walking toward the residence, the officer observed a pickup truck leaving. The officer waved his hands to tell the driver—the defendant—to stop. The officer intended to ask the defendant if he knew anything about the man with the outstanding warrants; the officer had no suspicion that the defendant was the man he was looking for or was engaged in criminal activity. The officer was in uniform but had no weapon drawn; his police vehicle was not blocking the road and neither his vehicle's blue lights nor sirens were activated. When the defendant stopped the vehicle, the officer almost immediately smelled an odor of alcohol from inside the vehicle. After the defendant admitted that he had been drinking, the officer arrested the defendant for impaired driving. Because a reasonable person would have felt free to decline the officer's request to stop, no seizure occurred; rather, the encounter was consensual.

**State v. Mangum,** ___ N.C. App. ___, 795 S.E.2d 106 (2016). In this impaired driving case, the court ruled that the defendant was not seized within the meaning of the Fourth Amendment until he submitted to the officer's authority by stopping his vehicle. The court rejected the defendant's argument that the seizure occurred when the officer activated his blue lights. Because the defendant continued driving after the blue lights were activated, there was no submission to the officer's authority and no seizure until the defendant stopped his vehicle. As a result, the reasonable suspicion inquiry can consider circumstances that arose after the officer's activation of his blue lights but before the defendant's submission to authority.

## The Authority to Make an Investigative Stop or Take Other Action without Reasonable Suspicion (page 161)

### Conducting Impaired-Driving and Driver's License Checkpoints (page 162)

#### NORTH CAROLINA COURT OF APPEALS (page 164)

**State v. Ashworth,** ___ N.C. App. ___, 790 S.E.2d 173 (2016). In this impaired driving case, the court ruled that the trial court erred by denying the defendant's motion to suppress, which had asserted that a checkpoint stop violated his constitutional rights. In a constitutional challenge to a checkpoint, a two-part inquiry applies: the court must first determine the primary programmatic purpose of the checkpoint; if a legitimate primary programmatic purpose is found, the court must judge its reasonableness. The defendant did not raise an issue about whether the checkpoint had a proper purpose. When determining reasonableness, a court must weigh the public's interest in the checkpoint against the individual's Fourth Amendment privacy interest, applying the *Brown v. Texas*, 443 U.S. 47 (1979), three-part test (gravity of the public concerns served by the seizure, the degree to which the seizure advances the public interest, and the severity of the interference with individual liberty) to this balancing inquiry. The court held that the trial court's findings of fact were insufficient to permit the trial court to meaningfully weigh the considerations required under the second and third prongs of the test. This constituted plain error. The court vacated the trial court's order denying the defendant's motion and remanded the case for further findings of fact and conclusions of law regarding the reasonableness of the checkpoint stop.

# The Authority to Arrest: Probable Cause (page 172)

## Determination of Probable Cause (page 172)

### UNITED STATES SUPREME COURT (page 172)

*District of Columbia v. Wesby,* 138 S. Ct. 577 (2018). Ruling in a civil suit against the District of Columbia and five of its police officers brought by individuals arrested for holding a raucous late-night party in a house they did not have permission to enter, the Court held that the officers had probable cause to arrest the party-goers and were entitled to qualified immunity. As to probable cause, the Court concluded that "[c]onsidering the totality of the circumstances, the officers made an entirely reasonable inference that the partygoers were knowingly taking advantage of a vacant house as a venue for their late-night party" (quotation omitted). In this respect, the Court noted the condition of the house, including, among other things, that multiple neighbors told the officers that the house had been vacant for several months and that the house had virtually no furniture and few signs of inhabitance. The Court also noted the partygoers' conduct, including, among other things, that the party was still going strong when the officers arrived after 1:00 a.m., with music so loud that it could be heard from outside; upon entering, multiple officers smelled marijuana; partygoers had left beer bottles and cups of liquor on the floor; the living room had been converted into a makeshift strip club; and the officers found upstairs a group of men with a single, naked woman on a bare mattress—the only bed in the house—along with multiple open condom wrappers and a used condom. The Court further noted the partygoers' reaction to the officers, including scattering and hiding at the sight of the uniformed officers. Finally, the Court noted the partygoers' vague and implausible answers to the officers' questions about who had given them permission to be at the house. The Court went on to hold that the officers were entitled to qualified immunity.

### NORTH CAROLINA COURT OF APPEALS (page 176)

*State v. Parisi,* ___ N.C. App. ___, ___ S.E.2d ___, 2018 WL 2626965 (June 5, 2018). In this impaired driving case, the court held, over a dissent, that an officer had probable cause to arrest the defendant for driving while impaired. The officer was operating a checkpoint. As a vehicle being driven by the defendant stopped at the checkpoint, the officer approached the driver's door and saw an open box of alcoholic beverage on the passenger floorboard but did not see any open containers. The defendant had glassy, watery eyes and smelled of alcohol. Upon inquiry, the defendant told the officer he had consumed three beers earlier that evening. The officer administered an HGN test and found that the defendant demonstrated six "clues" indicating impairment. The officer also administered a walk and turn test and the defendant missed multiple steps. Finally, when the officer administered a one-leg stand test, the defendant used his arms and swayed, indicators of impairment. These facts supported probable cause.

*State v. Clapp,* ___ N.C. App. ___, ___ S.E.2d ___, 2018 WL 2626889 (June 5, 2018). Probable cause supported the defendant's second arrest for impaired driving. After the defendant's first arrest for DWI, he signed a written promise to appear and was released. Thirty minutes later Officer Hall saw the defendant in the driver's seat of his vehicle at a gas station, with the engine running. The defendant had an odor of alcohol; slurred speech; and red, glassy eyes and was unsteady on his feet. The defendant told the officer that he was driving his vehicle to his son's residence. The officer did not perform field sobriety tests because the defendant was unable to safely stand on his feet. Based on the defendant's prior blood-alcohol reading—done less than two hours before the second incident—and the officer's training about the rate of alcohol elimination from the body, the officer formed the opinion that the defendant still had alcohol in his system. The defendant was arrested a second time for DWI and, because of his first arrest, also for driving while license revoked. The trial court granted the defendant's motion to suppress evidence in connection with his second arrest. The State appealed and the court of appeals reversed. The court began by determining that certain findings made by the trial court were not supported by competent evidence. The court then held that probable cause supported the defendant's second arrest. The defendant admitted that he drove his vehicle between his two encounters with the police. During the second encounter, Hall observed that the defendant had red, glassy eyes; an odor of alcohol; and slurred speech and was unsteady on his feet to the extent that it was unsafe to conduct field sobriety tests. While Hall did not observe the defendant's driving behavior, he had personal knowledge that the defendant had a blood alcohol concentration of .16 one hour and 40 minutes prior to the second encounter. And Hall testified that based on standard elimination rates of alcohol for an average individual, the defendant probably still would be impaired.

**State v. Daniel,** ___ N.C. App. ___, 814 S.E.2d 618 (2018). Over a dissent, the court held that because an officer had probable cause to arrest the defendant for impaired driving, the trial court erred by granting the defendant's motion to suppress. Here, the trooper "clocked" the defendant traveling at 80 m.p.h. in a 65 m.p.h. zone on a highway. As the trooper approached the defendant's vehicle, the defendant abruptly moved from the left lane of the highway into the right lane, nearly striking another vehicle before stopping on the shoulder. During the stop, the trooper noticed a moderate odor of alcohol emanating from the defendant and observed an open 24-ounce container of beer in the cup-holder next to the driver's seat. The defendant told the trooper that he had just purchased the beer and was drinking it while driving down the highway. The defendant admitted that he had been drinking heavily several hours before the encounter with the trooper. The trooper did not have the defendant perform any field sobriety tests but did ask the defendant to submit to two Alco-sensor tests, both of which yielded positive results for alcohol. The court noted that while swerving alone does not give rise to probable cause, additional factors creating dangerous circumstances may, as was the case here.

**State v. Wilkes,** ___ N.C. App. ___, 807 S.E.2d 672 (2017). The court ruled that officers had probable cause to arrest the defendant, and, thus, the trial court did not err by denying the defendant's motion to suppress incriminating statements made by the defendant after arrest. After law enforcement discovered a woman's body inside an abandoned, burned car, officers arrested the defendant. During questioning after arrest, the defendant implicated himself in the woman's murder. He unsuccessfully moved to suppress those incriminating statements and challenged the trial court's denial of his suppression motion on appeal. At the time the officers arrested the defendant, they had already visited the victim's home and found a knife on the chair near a window with the screen cut. When they questioned the victim's boyfriend, he admitted that he was with the defendant at the victim's home on the night of the murder and that, after the victim locked the two men out of her house, the boyfriend cut the screen, entered the house through the window, unlocked the door from the inside, and let the defendant in. These facts and circumstances constituted sufficient information that would lead a reasonable officer to believe that the defendant had committed a breaking and entering. Thus, regardless of whether the officers had probable cause to arrest the defendant for murder, they had probable cause to arrest the defendant for that lesser crime.

**State v. Messer,** ___ N.C. App. ___, 806 S.E.2d 315 (2017). In this armed robbery and murder case, the court ruled that the trial court did not err by concluding that law enforcement officers had probable cause to arrest the defendant. Among other things, the defendant placed a telephone call using the victim's cell phone about 20 minutes before the victim's death was reported to law enforcement, the defendant spent the previous night at the victim's residence, the victim's son had last seen his father with the defendant, the victim's Smith and Wesson revolver was missing and a Smith and Wesson revolver was found near the victim's body, and the defendant was seen on the day of the victim's death driving an automobile matching the description of one missing from the victim's used car lot.

**State v. Lindsey,** ___ N.C. App. ___, 791 S.E.2d 496 (2016). An officer had probable cause to arrest the defendant for DWI. After the officer stopped the defendant's vehicle, he smelled a moderate odor of alcohol coming from the defendant and noticed that the defendant's eyes were red and glassy. Upon administration of an HGN test, the officer observed five of six indicators of impairment. The defendant was unable to provide a breath sample for an Alco-Sensor, which the officer viewed as willful refusal. The defendant admitted that he had consumed three beers, though he said his last consumption was nine hours prior. The officer arrested the defendant for DWI. The court held: "Without even considering defendant's multiple failed attempts to provide an adequate breath sample on an [A]lco-sensor device, we hold the trial court's findings support its conclusion that there was probable cause to arrest defendant for DWI."

**State v. Williams,** ___ N.C. App. ___, 786 S.E.2d 419 (2016). An officer had probable cause to arrest the defendant for DWI. The officer responded to a call involving operation of a golf cart and serious injury to an individual. The defendant admitted to the officer that he was the driver of the golf cart. The defendant had "very red and glassy" eyes and "a strong odor of alcohol coming from his breath." The defendant's clothes were bloody, and he was very talkative, repeating himself several times. The defendant's mannerisms were "fairly slow" and he placed a hand on the deputy's patrol car to maintain his balance. The defendant stated that he had "6 beers since noon" and submitted to an Alco-Sensor test, which was positive for alcohol.

## Objective Standard in Determining Reasonable Suspicion, Probable Cause, or the Fact of Arrest (page 182)
**NORTH CAROLINA SUPREME COURT** (page 182)

**State v. Nicholson,** ___ N.C. ___, 813 S.E.2d 840 (2018). Finding that the court of appeals placed undue weight on an officer's subjective interpretation of the facts (the officer's testimony suggested that he did not believe he had reasonable suspicion of criminal activity) rather than focusing on how an objective, reasonable officer would have viewed them, the court noted that an action is reasonable under the Fourth Amendment regardless of the officer's state of mind, if the circumstances viewed objectively justify the action.

# The Arrest Procedure (page 185)
**Entrance onto Premises to Arrest** (page 186)
*Exigent Circumstances* (page 188)
**NORTH CAROLINA COURT OF APPEALS** (page 189)

**State v. Adams,** ___ N.C. App. ___, 794 S.E.2d 357 (2016). The court ruled that exigent circumstances justified the officers' warrantless entry into the defendant's home to arrest him. It was undisputed that the officers had reasonable suspicion to stop the defendant for driving while license revoked. They pulled into the defendant's driveway behind him and activated blue lights as the defendant was exiting his vehicle and making his way toward his front door. The defendant did not stop for the blue lights and continued hurriedly toward the front door after the officers told him to stop. "At that point," the court explained, "the officers had probable cause to arrest defendant for resisting a public officer and began a 'hot pursuit' of defendant." The officers arrived at the front door just as the defendant was making his way across the threshold and were able to prevent him from closing the door. The officers then forced the front door open and detained and arrested the defendant just inside the door. The court held that the warrantless entry and arrest was proper under *United States v. Santana*, 427 U.S. 38 (1976). It explained: Hot pursuit has been recognized as an exigent circumstance sufficient to justify a warrantless entry into a residence where there is probable cause, without consideration of immediate danger or destruction of evidence.

# Law of Search and Seizure

## Introduction (page 195)

***Footnote 3*** (page 195)

In *State v. Terrell*,[1] the North Carolina Court of Appeals ruled that an officer exceeded the scope of a private search while examining a thumb drive. The defendant's girlfriend contacted law enforcement after seeing an image of a partly nude child on the drive. An officer subsequently searched the drive, looking for the image in question but discovering while doing so images of other nude minors the girlfriend never saw. The court of appeals ruled that the officer's warrantless examination of the additional images was an unlawful search. Citing *Riley v. California*,[2] the court ruled that an electronic storage device should not be viewed as a single container for Fourth Amendment purposes, and that the defendant retained an expectation of privacy in the information not examined by his girlfriend. As of this writing, the court's ruling has been stayed by the state supreme court, so further review is possible.[3]

## Observations and Actions That May Not Implicate Fourth Amendment Rights (page 196)

### NEW SECTION: Searches of Stolen or Misappropriated Property

A person does not have a reasonable expectation of privacy in stolen property and so cannot contest an officer's search of such property.[4] However, the United States Supreme Court recently ruled that a person driving a rental car may have a reasonable expectation of privacy in the vehicle even if the person is not listed as an authorized driver on the rental agreement; such a person is not necessarily in the same position as a thief. In *Byrd v. United States*,[5] the Court considered a driver who had been entrusted with a vehicle by a friend who was the only person listed on the rental agreement. The Court stated that "as a general rule, someone in otherwise lawful possession and control of a rental car has a reasonable expectation of privacy in it even if the rental agreement does not list him or her as an authorized driver."[6] Such a person would have a "right to

---

1. ___ N.C. App. ___, 810 S.E.2d 719, *temp. stay allowed*, ___ N.C. ___, 809 S.E.2d 499 (2018).

2. 573 U.S. ___, 134 S. Ct. 2473 (2014) (ruling that a search incident to arrest should not extend to digital data on cell phones).

3. For a discussion of *Terrell*, see Shea Denning, State v. Terrell *and the Private Search Doctrine*, UNC Sch. of Gov't: N.C. Crim. L. Blog (Feb. 7, 2018), https://nccriminallaw.sog.unc.edu/state-v-terrell-private-search-doctrine/.

4. *See, e.g.,* State v. White, 311 N.C. 238, 244 (1984) ("Defendant also challenges the search of the vehicle by law enforcement officers without a warrant. The record discloses that the vehicle in question was in fact stolen. Defendant presented no evidence showing any legitimate property or possessory interest in the automobile. The law is well settled in this jurisdiction that one has no standing to 'object to a search or seizure of the premises or property of another.'") (citation omitted).

5. 584 U.S. ___, 138 S. Ct. 1518 (2018).

6. *Id.* at ___, 138 S. Ct. at 1524.

exclude" others from the vehicle, such as potential carjackers, and would be able to contest a law enforcement search of the vehicle.[7]

### Areas Outside the Home: Curtilage and Open Fields (page 200)
*Common Entranceway to Residence* (page 203)

In *State v. Stanley*,[8] the court of appeals ruled that officers violated the Fourth Amendment by conducting a knock and talk at the back door of a residence, even though a gravel driveway "led to the back of the apartment" and a confidential informant had used the back door three times to make controlled buys at the property. The court emphasized that the front door is the entry normally used by social visitors, and stated that only in "unusual circumstances," not present here, would an officer be justified in approaching a side door or back door for a knock and talk. Although the informant used the back door several times, "the fact that the resident of a home may choose to allow certain individuals to use a back or side door does not mean that similar permission is deemed to have been given generally to members of the public."[9] The court's statements regarding the usual impermissibility of approaching a side door to a residence may call into question the suggestion in the final paragraph of this section of the main text that ordinarily a knock and talk may be conducted at either a front or a side door.

### Plain View Sensory Perceptions (Observation, Smell, Sound, Touch, and Taste) (page 203)
*Use of Special Devices or Animals* (page 207)

**Aircraft** (page 207)

Law enforcement agencies are increasingly relying on drones, rather than traditional aircraft, to conduct aerial overflights and surveillance. North Carolina statutory law requires an officer to obtain a warrant before using a drone to conduct surveillance of a person, a dwelling, or curtilage, absent consent or exigency.[10]

**Dogs** (page 209)

Although the use of a dog during a traffic stop is not itself a search and does not itself invade a motorist's reasonable expectation of privacy, it is important to remember that, under *Rodriguez v. United States*,[11] the use of the dog may not extend the duration of the stop absent consent or reasonable suspicion.

## Wiretapping, Eavesdropping, Access to Stored Electronic Communications, and Related Issues (page 210)
### Access to Real-Time (Prospective) or Historical Cell-Site Location Information (page 220)

The United States Supreme Court ruled in *Carpenter v. United States*[12] that "when the Government accessed [many days' worth of historical cell site location information] from [a suspect's] wireless carriers, it invaded [his] reasonable expectation of privacy in the whole of his physical movements," and so conducted a search for purposes of the Fourth Amendment. The Court stated that investigators "must generally obtain a warrant

---

7. For a complete discussion of *Byrd*, see Jeff Welty, *Supreme Court: Driver of Rental Car, Not Listed on Rental Agreement, Has Reasonable Expectation of Privacy*, UNC SCH. OF GOV'T: N.C. CRIM. L. BLOG (May 21, 2018), https://nccriminallaw.sog.unc.edu/supreme-court-driver-of-rental-car-not-listed-on-rental-agreement-has-reasonable-expectation-of-privacy/.

8. ___ N.C. App. ___, ___ S.E.2d ___, 2018 WL 2207928 (May 15, 2018).

9. *Id.* at ___, ___ S.E. 2d at ___, 2018 WL 2207928 at *6.

10. *See* G.S. 15A-300.1. For a discussion of the various legal constraints and considerations involved in law enforcement use of drones, see Jeff Welty, *Update on Drones*, UNC SCH. OF GOV'T: N.C. CRIM. L. BLOG (Aug. 22, 2017), https://nccriminallaw.sog.unc.edu/update-on-drones/.

11. 575 U.S. ___, 135 S. Ct. 1609 (2015).

12. ___ U.S. ___, 138 S. Ct. 2206 (2018).

supported by probable cause before acquiring such records,"[13] unless an exception to the warrant requirement is present, such as exigency. This effectively overrules the *Perry* decision noted in the main volume, as well as the similar decisions of many other lower courts.[14] It also effectively prohibits officers from using a "reasonable grounds" court order under 18 U.S.C. § 2703(d) to obtain long-term historical cell site location information.

*Carpenter* does not address all the legal issues concerning cell phones and location information. The majority expressly declined to opine about the Fourth Amendment status of "real-time CSLI [(cell-site location information)] or 'tower dumps,'" and left open the possibility that obtaining only short-term historical CSLI would not be a search.[15] A cautious officer seeking CSLI or other phone-related location information, even information not directly governed by the holding in *Carpenter*, may wish to use a search warrant or the functional equivalent, such as a court order based on full probable cause, to do so.[16]

## Bank Records (page 222)

The State Bar has determined that only a prosecutor, not an officer, may file a motion with a court for an order seeking financial records. The State Bar cautioned an officer who filed such a motion, concluding that the officer engaged in the unauthorized practice of law by doing so.[17]

## Search and Seizure by Valid Consent (page 224)

### Content of a Valid Consent (page 229)

#### *Voluntariness of the Expression* (page 229)

The potential for an officer's actions to generate unlawful coercion is illustrated by the recent case of *State v. Miller*,[18] where the North Carolina Court of Appeals ruled that an officer engaged in coercion that rendered a suspect's consent to search his vehicle involuntary. After stopping a vehicle for motor vehicle violations, the officer came to suspect that the vehicle's occupants were involved in drug activity. The officer had the defendant, who had been driving, get out of the vehicle, then turn so that he was facing the rear of the vehicle with his arms and legs spread, and then asked for the defendant's consent to search the vehicle. Assuming that the defendant consented, the court concluded that any consent was not voluntary: "[T]his was textbook coercion. . . .[I]t was certainly not a free and intelligent waiver of [the defendant's] constitutional rights."[19] On

---

13. *Id.* at ___, 138 S. Ct. at 2221.

14. *See, e.g.*, United States v. Riley, 858 F.3d 1012 (6th Cir. 2017) (ruling that "tracking [a robbery defendant's] real-time GPS location data for approximately seven hours preceding his arrest . . . did not amount to a Fourth Amendment search" and therefore did not require probable cause).

15. *Carpenter*, ___ U.S. at ___, 138 S. Ct. at 2220. For a detailed discussion of *Carpenter*, see Jeff Welty, *Supreme Court Rules that Obtaining Cell Site Location Information Is a Search*, UNC Sch. of Gov't: N.C. Crim. L. Blog (June 25, 2018), https://nccriminallaw.sog.unc.edu/9411-2/.

16. For a further discussion of whether a court order based on probable cause may be used in place of a search warrant, see Jeff Welty, *Carpenter, Search Warrants, and Court Orders Based on Probable Cause*, UNC Sch. of Gov't: N.C. Crim. L. Blog (July 30, 2018), https://nccriminallaw.sog.unc.edu/carpenter-search-warrants-and-court-orders-based-on-probable-cause/.

17. For a complete discussion of the unauthorized practice issue, and to see a copy of the State Bar's letter, see Jeff Welty, *Officers' Applications for Investigative Orders and the Unauthorized Practice of Law*, UNC Sch. of Gov't: N.C. Crim. L. Blog (May 7, 2018), https://nccriminallaw.sog.unc.edu/officers-applications-for-investigative-orders-and-the-unauthorized-practice-of-law/.

18. ___ N.C. App. ___, 795 S.E.2d 374 (2016), *rev'd on other grounds*, ___ N.C. ___, 814 S.E.2d 81 (2018).

19. *Id.* at ___, 795 S.E. 2d at 379.

further review, however, the state supreme court ruled that the defendant waived his Fourth Amendment claim by failing to raise it in superior court; the court therefore did not reach the merits of the issue.

If a person has been unlawfully detained, any consent to search given during the unlawful detention is likely to be deemed invalid, either as involuntary or as tainted fruit of the detention.[20]

## Invasion of Privacy by a Search or Seizure with Sufficient Reason (page 233)
### Search and Seizure of Evidence with Probable Cause (page 234)
#### *Search and Seizure of Vehicles with Probable Cause* (page 236)

In *Collins v. Virginia*,[21] the United States Supreme Court ruled that the automobile exception to the warrant requirement does not permit an officer, uninvited and without a warrant, to enter the curtilage of a home to search a vehicle parked there. The Court stated that "the scope of the automobile exception extends no further than the automobile itself."[22] It rejected Virginia's request that it expand the scope of the automobile exception to permit police to access an automobile to carry out a search even if the Fourth Amendment protects the area through which the officer would need to travel to reach the vehicle:

> Just as an officer must have a lawful right of access to any contraband he discovers in plain view in order to seize it without a warrant, and just as an officer must have a lawful right of access in order to arrest a person in his home, so, too, an officer must have a lawful right of access to a vehicle in order to search it pursuant to the automobile exception. The automobile exception does not afford the necessary lawful right of access to search a vehicle parked within a home or its curtilage because it does not justify an intrusion on a person's separate and substantial Fourth Amendment interest in his home and curtilage.[23]

#### *Search of a Person for Evidence with Probable Cause* (page 245)
##### Probable cause to arrest and to search (page 245)

In *State v. Pigford*,[24] the defendant was driving a vehicle that was stopped at a checkpoint. A passenger was sitting in the front seat. The officer smelled an odor of marijuana coming from the vehicle but was unable to establish the exact location of the odor. The officer ordered the defendant out of the vehicle and searched him, finding cocaine and other items. The state court of appeals found the search of the defendant unjustified, as there was no evidence that the odor was personally attributable to the defendant. When an officer smells an odor of marijuana coming from a vehicle, the vehicle itself may be searched under the automobile exception to the warrant requirement, but the odor does not automatically provide an officer with probable cause to conduct an immediate warrantless search of the driver.[25]

---

20. *See* Florida v. Royer, 460 U.S. 491 (1983) ("Because . . . Royer was being illegally detained when he consented to the search of his luggage . . . the consent was tainted by the illegality and was ineffective to justify the search."); State v. Parker, ___ N.C. App. ___, ___, 807 S.E.2d 617, 622 (2017) (ruling that "defendant's consent to search his person, given during the period of unreasonable detention, was not voluntary").

21. 584 U.S. ___, 138 S. Ct. 1663 (2018).

22. *Id.* at ___, 138 S. Ct. at 1667.

23. *Id.* at ___, 138 S. Ct. at 1672.

24. ___ N.C. App. ___, 789 S.E.2d 857 (2016).

25. For a further discussion of *Pigford* and other cases concerning searches of vehicles and their occupants based on an officer's detection of the odor of marijuana, see Jeff Welty, *Searches of Vehicles and Occupants Based on the Odor of Marijuana*, UNC Sch. of Gov't: N.C. Crim. L. Blog (Sept. 19, 2016), https://nccriminallaw.sog.unc.edu/searches-vehicles-occupants-based-odor-marijuana/.

**Obtaining a blood sample when an impaired driver refuses a chemical test** (page 245)

The North Carolina Court of Appeals applied *McNeely* in *State v. Burris*,[26] finding sufficient exigency to support a warrantless blood draw. The defendant refused to take a breath test, and the officer estimated that it would take an hour and a half to get a search warrant given the limited number of officers available to assist and the distance to the magistrate's office. A roadside test had indicated that the defendant's BAC was .10, so the officer reasonably believed that the delay would result in the dissipation of alcohol in the defendant's blood.

A further consequence of *McNeely* and *Birchfield v. North Dakota*[27] is that blood may not automatically be drawn from an unconscious motorist suspected of impaired driving. The North Carolina Supreme Court so held in *State v. Romano*,[28] declaring Chapter 20, Section 16.2(b), of the North Carolina General Statutes (hereinafter, G.S.) (allowing blood draw from an unconscious person) unconstitutional as applied to the defendant in that case:

> Here there is no dispute that the officer did not get a warrant and that there were no exigent circumstances. Regarding consent, the State's argument was based solely on [G.S.] 20-16.2(b) as a per se exception to the warrant requirement. To be sure, the implied-consent statute, as well as a person's decision to drive on public roads, are factors to consider when analyzing whether a suspect has consented to a blood draw, but the statute alone does not create a per se exception to the warrant requirement. The State did not present any other evidence of consent or argue that under the totality of the circumstances defendant consented to a blood draw. Therefore, the State did not carry its burden of proving voluntary consent.[29]

## Search and Seizure to Protect Officers, Other People, or Property (page 249)

### *Search Incident to Arrest* (page 249)

#### Strip searches and body-cavity searches (page 253)

In *State v. Fuller*,[30] the North Carolina Court of Appeals determined that a search of the defendant's person was a proper search incident to his arrest. An officer stopped the defendant's vehicle for driving with a revoked license and arrested the defendant. The officer then conducted a consent search of the vehicle, which failed to locate any contraband. However, a K-9 dog arrived and "hit" on the driver's seat cushion. When a further search uncovered no contraband or narcotics, the officer concluded that the narcotics must be on the defendant's person. The defendant was brought to the police department and was searched. The search involved lowering the defendant's pants and long johns to his knees. During the search the officer pulled out, but did not pull down, the defendant's underwear and observed the defendant's genitals and buttocks. Cocaine eventually was retrieved from a hidden area on the fly of the defendant's pants. The court of appeals rejected the defendant's argument that the strip search could only have been conducted with probable cause and exigent circumstances, noting that the exigency standard applies only to roadside strip searches. Here, the search was conducted incident to the defendant's lawful arrest and inside a private interview room at a police facility. Furthermore, the scope of the search was reasonable. It was limited to the area of the defendant's body and

---

26. ___ N.C. App. ___, 799 S.E.2d 452 (2017).

27. 579 U.S. ___, 136 S. Ct. 2160 (2016) (ruling that the search incident to arrest doctrine does not justify the warrantless taking of a blood sample, and that "motorists cannot be deemed to have consented to submit to a blood test on pain of committing a criminal offense" as North Dakota's law provided).

28. 369 N.C. 678 (2017). For a discussion of *Romano* and related issues, see Shea Denning, *State Supreme Court Issues Significant Rulings on HGN Evidence and Blood Draws in DWI Cases*, UNC SCH. OF GOV'T: N.C. CRIM. L. BLOG (June 14, 2017), https://nccriminallaw.sog.unc.edu/state-supreme-court-issues-significant-rulings-hgn-evidence-blood-draws-dwi-cases/.

29. *Romano*, 369 N.C. at 692.

30. ___ N.C. App. ___, 809 S.E.2d 157 (2017).

clothing that would have come in contact with the cushion of the driver's seat where the dog alerted, and the defendant was searched inside a private interview room at the police station with only the defendant and two officers present. The officers did not remove the defendant's clothing above the waist. They did not fully remove his undergarments, nor did they touch his genitals or any body cavity. The court thus concluded that the place, manner, justification, and scope of the search of the defendant's person were reasonable.

# Chapter 3 Appendix: Case Summaries

## Search and Seizure Issues (page 275)

## Observations and Actions That May Not Implicate Fourth Amendment Rights
(page 280)
### Private Search or Seizure (page 280)
**NORTH CAROLINA COURT OF APPEALS** (page 281)

*State v. Terrell*, ___ N.C. App. ___, 810 S.E.2d 719, *temp. stay allowed*, ___ N.C. ___, 809 S.E.2d 499 (2018). In this peeping and sexual exploitation of a minor case, and with one judge dissenting in part, the court held that the trial court erred by concluding that an officer's warrantless search of the defendant's thumb drive was lawful. While examining a thumb drive belonging to the defendant, the defendant's girlfriend saw an image of her nine-year-old granddaughter sleeping without a shirt. Believing the image was inappropriate, she contacted law enforcement and gave them the thumb drive. The thumb drive was placed in an evidence locker. Later, an officer conducted a warrantless search of the thumb drive to locate the image in question. During this search he discovered images of other partially or fully nude minors that the girlfriend never saw. Using this information in a warrant application, the officer obtained a search warrant to forensically examine the contents of the thumb drive for "contraband images of child pornography and evidence of additional victims and crimes." The executed warrant yielded 12 incriminating images located in a different subfolder than the original image. After the defendant was charged, he unsuccessfully moved to suppress the contents of the thumb drive. The trial court determined that the girlfriend's private viewing of the thumb drive defeated the defendant's expectation of privacy in its contents and thus that the officer's warrantless search was lawful under the private search exception to the warrant requirement. After conviction, the defendant appealed. The court held that the trial court erred by concluding that the girlfriend's thumb drive search effectively frustrated the defendant's expectation of privacy in its entire contents. Distinguishing a prior ruling in a case involving a videotape and citing *Riley v. California*, 573 U.S. ___, 134 S. Ct. 2473 (2014) (declining to extend the search-incident-to-arrest doctrine to digital data on cell phones), the court found that with respect to this search of digital data on an electronic storage device, the defendant retained an expectation of privacy in the information not revealed by his girlfriend's search. In so ruling the court held that an electronic storage device should not be viewed as a single container for Fourth Amendment purposes. It then turned to whether the trial court's findings supported its conclusion that the officer's search remained within the permissible scope of the girlfriend's prior search and whether it was reasonable under the circumstances, and was, therefore, a valid warrantless search under the private-search doctrine. In this respect it held: The officer's warrantless search was not authorized under the private-search doctrine, since the trial court's findings establish that he did not conduct his warrantless search with the requisite "virtual certainty" that the thumb drive contained only contraband, or that his inspection of its data would not reveal anything more than what the girlfriend already told him. However, finding the record insufficient to determine whether the trial court would have determined that the search warrant was supported by probable cause without the tainted evidence from the unlawful search, the court remanded to the trial court to determine the validity of the search warrant. As of this writing, this decision has been stayed by the state supreme court.

## Areas outside the Home: Curtilage and Open Fields (page 287)

### UNITED STATES SUPREME COURT (page 287)

*Collins v. Virginia,* 584 U.S. ___, 138 S. Ct. 1663 (2018). In the course of deciding whether an officer's warrantless search of a motorcycle parked in the driveway of a home was justified under the automobile exception, the Court considered whether the motorcycle was parked within the curtilage of the dwelling. It ruled that it was. The motorcycle was parked at the end of the driveway, which terminated next to the house. The parking area was "enclosed on two sides by a brick wall about the height of a car and on a third side by the house. A side door provide[d] direct access between this partially enclosed section of the driveway and the house. A visitor endeavoring to reach the front door of the house would have to walk partway up the driveway, but would turn off before entering the enclosure and instead proceed up a set of steps leading to the front porch." On these facts, the Court had no difficulty concluding that the motorcycle was parked within the curtilage.

### NORTH CAROLINA COURT OF APPEALS (page 290)

*State v. Stanley*, ___ N.C. App. ___, ___ S.E.2d ___, 2018 WL 2207928 (May 15, 2018). The knock and talk conducted by officers in this drug case violated the Fourth Amendment. After a confidential informant notified officers that he had purchased heroin from a person at an apartment, officers conducted three controlled drug buys at the apartment. On all three occasions the purchases were made at the back door of the apartment from an individual named Meager, who did not live there. Officers then obtained a warrant for Meager's arrest and approached the apartment to serve him. Upon arrival, they immediately walked down the driveway that led to the back of the apartment and knocked on the door. Events then transpired which lead to, among other things, a pat-down of the defendant and the discovery of controlled substances on the defendant's person. The defendant was arrested and charged with drug offenses. He filed a motion to suppress. When it was denied, he pled guilty, reserving his right to appeal. On appeal, the court agreed that the knock and talk was unlawful. It held that "to pass constitutional muster the officers were required to conduct the knock and talk by going to the front door, which they did not do. Rather than using the paved walkway that led directly to the unobstructed front door, they walked along the gravel driveway into the backyard to knock on the back door, which was not visible from the street. This was unreasonable." The court rejected the trial court's determination that the officers had an implied license to approach the back door because the confidential informant had purchased drugs there. The court stated that "the fact that the resident of a home may choose to allow certain individuals to use a back or side door does not mean that similar permission is deemed to have been given generally to members of the public." The court recognized that "unusual circumstances in some cases may allow officers to lawfully approach a door of the residence other than the front door in order to conduct a knock and talk." However no such unusual circumstances were presented in this case.

*State v. Huddy*, ___ N.C. App. ___, 799 S.E.2d 650 (2017). An officer violated the defendant's Fourth Amendment rights by searching the curtilage of his home without a warrant. The officer saw a vehicle with its doors open at the back of a 150-yard driveway leading to the defendant's home. Concerned that the vehicle might be part of a break-in or home invasion, the officer drove down the driveway, ran the vehicle's tags, checked—but did not knock—on the front door, checked the windows and doors of the home for signs of forced entry, "cleared" the sides of the house, and then went through a closed gate in a chain-link fence enclosing the home's backyard and approached the storm door at the back of the house. As the officer approached the door, which was not visible from the street, he smelled marijuana, which led to the defendant's arrest for drug charges. The State relied on two exceptions to the warrant requirement in attempting to justify the officer's search of the curtilage: the knock and talk doctrine and the community caretaking doctrine. The court found, however, that neither exception applied. First, the officer did more than merely knock and talk. Specifically, he ran a license plate not visible from the street, walked around the house examining windows and searching for signs of a break-in, and went to a rear door not visible from the street and located behind a closed gate. Likewise, the court ruled that the community caretaking doctrine did not support the officer's actions: "The presence of a vehicle in one's driveway with its doors open is not the sort of emergency that justifies the community caretaker exception." The court also noted that because the Fourth Amendment's protections "are at their very strongest within one's home," the public need justifying the community caretaking exception "must be particularly strong to justify a warrantless search of a home."

**State v. Kirkman**, ___ N.C. App. ___, 795 S.E.2d 379 (2016). In this drug case, an officer lawfully approached the front of the defendant's home and obtained information later used to procure a search warrant. Specifically, he heard a generator and noticed condensation and mold, factors that in his experience and training were consistent with the indoor cultivation of marijuana. The court stated that "[i]t is well-established that an officer may approach the front door of a home, and if he is able to observe conditions from that position which indicate illegal activity, it is completely proper for him to act upon that information."

## Plain View (Sensory Perception) (page 297)
### NORTH CAROLINA COURT OF APPEALS (page 301)

**State v. Smith**, ___ N.C. App. ___, 804 S.E.2d 235, *review allowed*, ___ N.C. ___, 807 S.E.2d 575 (2017). Three officers entered the defendant's apartment to execute arrest warrants issued for misdemeanors. While two officers made the in-home arrest, the third conducted a protective sweep of the defendant's apartment. A shotgun was leaning against the wall in the entry of the defendant's bedroom. The bedroom door was open and the shotgun was visible, in plain view, from the hallway. The officer walked past the shotgun when checking the defendant's bedroom to confirm that no other occupants were present. After completing the sweep, the officer secured the shotgun "to have it in . . . control and also check to see if it was stolen." The officer located the serial number on the shotgun and called it into the police department, which reported that the gun was stolen. The officer then seized the weapon. The defendant moved to suppress the shotgun, arguing that the officer lacked authority to conduct a protective sweep and that the seizure could not be justified under the plain view doctrine. The trial court denied the defendant's motion to suppress. After determining that the protective sweep was proper, because the rooms in the apartment all adjoined the place of arrest and were locations from which an attack could be immediately launched, the court considered the seizure of the shotgun. Over a dissent, the court held that the plain view doctrine could not justify seizure of the shotgun. The court agreed with the defendant that the incriminating nature of the shotgun was not immediately apparent and that the officer conducted an unlawful search by manipulating the shotgun to reveal its serial number. The court emphasized that the officers were executing arrest warrants for misdemeanor offenses and were not aware that the defendant was a convicted felon. Before the seizure, the officer asked the other officers in the apartment if the defendant was a convicted felon, which they could not confirm. The court went on to find that the incriminating character of the shotgun became apparent only upon some further action by the officers—here, exposing its serial number and calling that number into the police department. Such action constitutes a search, separate and apart from the lawful objective of the entry. No evidence indicated that the officer had probable cause to believe that the shotgun was stolen at the time of the search. This case is currently before the North Carolina Supreme Court for its review.

## Historical Cell-Site Information (page 308)
### UNITED STATES SUPREME COURT (page 308)

**Carpenter v. United States**, ___ U.S. ___, 138 S.Ct. 2206 (2018). The court ruled that "when the Government accessed [many days' worth of historical cell-site location information] from [a robbery suspect's] wireless carriers, it invaded [his] reasonable expectation of privacy in the whole of his physical movements," and so conducted a search for purposes of the Fourth Amendment. The Court stated that investigators "must generally obtain a warrant supported by probable cause before acquiring such records," unless an exception to the warrant requirement, such as exigency, is present. This effectively overrules prior North Carolina precedent and prohibits officers from using "reasonable grounds" court orders under 18 U.S.C. § 2703(d) to obtain long-term historical CSLI (cell-site location information). *Carpenter* does not, however, address all the legal issues concerning cell phones and location information. For example, the majority expressly declined to opine about the Fourth Amendment status of "real-time CSLI or 'tower dumps,'" and left open the possibility that obtaining only short-term historical CSLI would not be a search. For a detailed discussion of *Carpenter*, see Jeff Welty, *Supreme Court Rules that Obtaining Cell Site Location Information Is a Search*, UNC Sch. of Gov't: N.C. Crim. L. Blog (June 25, 2018), https://nccriminallaw.sog.unc.edu/9411-2/.

## Search and Seizure by Valid Consent (page 316)

### Voluntariness (page 316)

#### *Generally* (page 316)

**NORTH CAROLINA COURT OF APPEALS** (page 319)

*State v. Parker*, ___ N.C. App. ___, 807 S.E.2d 617 (2017). The defendant's consent to search his person was not voluntary where it was given during a period of unlawful detention. Believing that a confrontation between the defendant and a woman was going to escalate into a fight after observing the two yelling at each other in a driveway, officers approached and asked for the defendant's identification. In the process of de-escalating the situation, an officer checked the defendant's record and verified that he had no pending warrants. Without returning his identification, the officer asked for and received the defendant's consent to search his person. The court determined that under these circumstances the defendant's consent was not given voluntarily, reasoning that the officers unlawfully detained the defendant by retaining his identification after they had satisfied the purpose of the initial detention.

*State v. Miller*, ___ N.C. App. ___, 795 S.E.2d 374 (2016), *review allowed*, 370 N.C. 64 (2017). Even assuming that the traffic stop was lawful up to the point when the defendant consented to the search, his consent was not valid. Although the officer testified that the defendant verbally agreed to the search, footage from the body camera revealed a different version of the interaction. Specifically, the officer had the defendant turned around, facing the rear of the vehicle with his arms and legs spread, before he asked for his consent. The court concluded: "[T]his was textbook coercion. If defendant did respond to Officer Harris's request—and it is still not apparent that he did—it was certainly not a free and intelligent waiver of his constitutional rights." The State's petition to review this ruling has been allowed.

*State v. Cobb*, ___ N.C. App. ___, 789 S.E.2d 532 (2016). In this drug case, the court held that the defendant's consent to search his room in a rooming house was voluntarily given. The court rejected the defendant's argument that he was in custody when consent was given. There was no evidence that the defendant's movements were limited by the officers during the encounter. Also, the officers did not supervise the defendant while they were in the home; rather, they simply followed the defendant to his room after he gave consent to search.

### Scope of the Search (page 324)

**NORTH CAROLINA COURT OF APPEALS** (page 325)

*State v. Bullock*, ___ N.C. App. ___, 811 S.E.2d 713 (2018). During a traffic stop, the defendant consented to a search of the vehicle but not to a search of his personal belongings in it, a bag and two hoodies. After searching the vehicle, the officer's K-9—which had failed to alert to the vehicle—alerted to the presence of narcotics in the defendant's bag, which had been removed from the vehicle before the search began. The scope of the officer's search of the vehicle did not exceed the scope of the defendant's consent. Furthermore, the defendant did not revoke consent to search his vehicle. Although the defendant asked the officer what would happen if he revoked his consent, the defendant never revoked consent to search the vehicle, even after the officer explained that he needed to wait for a second officer to arrive to conduct the search.

# Search and Seizure of Evidence with Probable Cause, Reasonable Suspicion, or Other Justification (page 336)

## Vehicles, Including Containers within Vehicles (page 336)

### *Generally* (page 336)

#### UNITED STATES SUPREME COURT (page 336)

*Collins v. Virginia,* 584 U.S. ___, 138 S. Ct. 1663 (2018). The automobile exception to the Fourth Amendment does not permit an officer, uninvited and without a warrant, to enter the curtilage of a home to search a vehicle parked there. In this case, an officer saw the driver of an orange and black motorcycle with an extended frame commit a traffic infraction. The driver eluded the officer's attempt to stop the motorcycle. A few weeks later, another officer saw a similar motorcycle traveling well over the speed limit, but the driver got away from him, too. The officers compared notes, determined that the two incidents involved the same motorcyclist, and that the motorcycle likely was stolen and in the possession of Ryan Collins. After discovering photographs on Collins's Facebook page showing an orange and black motorcycle parked at the top of the driveway of a house, one of the officers tracked down the address of the house, drove there, and parked on the street. It was later established that Collins's girlfriend lived in the house and that Collins stayed there a few nights per week. From the street, the officer saw what appeared to be the motorcycle in question. The officer, who did not have a warrant, walked toward the house. He stopped to take a photograph of the covered motorcycle from the sidewalk, and then walked onto the residential property and up to the top of the driveway where the motorcycle was parked. He removed the tarp, revealing a motorcycle that looked like the one from the speeding incident. He ran a search of the license plate and vehicle identification numbers, which confirmed that the motorcycle was stolen. The officer photographed the uncovered motorcycle, put the tarp back on, left the property, and returned to his car to wait for the defendant. The defendant was ultimately arrested, and he unsuccessfully sought to suppress the evidence the officer obtained as a result of the warrantless search of the motorcycle. The Supreme Court granted certiorari and reversed. The Court characterized the case as arising "at the intersection of two components of the Court's Fourth Amendment jurisprudence: the automobile exception to the warrant requirement and the protection extended to the curtilage of a home." After reviewing the law on these doctrines, the Court turned to whether the location in question is curtilage. It noted that according to photographs in the record, the driveway runs alongside the front lawn and up a few yards past the front perimeter of the house. The top portion of the driveway that sits behind the front perimeter of the house is enclosed on two sides by a brick wall about the height of a car and on a third side by the house. A side door provides direct access between this partially enclosed section of the driveway and the house. A visitor endeavoring to reach the front door would have to walk partway up the driveway, but would turn off before entering the enclosure and instead proceed up a set of steps leading to the front porch. When the officer searched the motorcycle, it was parked inside this partially enclosed top portion of the driveway that abuts the house. The Court concluded that the driveway was properly considered curtilage. The Court continued, noting that by physically intruding on the curtilage, the officer not only invaded the defendant's Fourth Amendment interest in the item searched—the motorcycle—but also his interest in the curtilage of the home at which he was a guest. Finding the case an "easy" one, the Court concluded that the automobile exception did not justify an invasion of the curtilage. It clarified that "the scope of the automobile exception extends no further than the automobile itself." The Court rejected Virginia's request that it expand the scope of the automobile exception to permit police to invade any space outside an automobile even if the Fourth Amendment protects that space. It continued:

> Just as an officer must have a lawful right of access to any contraband he discovers in plain view in order to seize it without a warrant, and just as an officer must have a lawful right of access in order to arrest a person in his home, so, too, an officer must have a lawful right of access to a vehicle in order to search it pursuant to the automobile exception. The automobile exception does not afford the

necessary lawful right of access to search a vehicle parked within a home or its curtilage because it does not justify an intrusion on a person's separate and substantial Fourth Amendment interest in his home and curtilage.

The Court summed up that "the automobile exception does not permit an officer without a warrant to enter a home or its curtilage in order to search a vehicle therein." It left for resolution on remand whether the officer's warrantless intrusion on the curtilage may have been reasonable on a different basis, such as the exigent circumstances exception to the warrant requirement.

### NORTH CAROLINA COURT OF APPEALS (page 339)

**State v. Burton**, ___ N.C. App. ___, 796 S.E.2d 65 (2017). The court rejected the defendant's claim that counsel was ineffective by failing to object to the admission of cocaine found during an officer's warrantless search of the defendant's vehicle; the court rejected the defendant's argument that the State was required to prove that the defendant's car was "readily mobile" in order for the automobile exception to the warrant requirement to apply. An officer searched the vehicle after smelling a strong odor of marijuana and seeing an individual sitting in the passenger seat with marijuana on his lap. The cocaine was found during a subsequent search of the vehicle. The vehicle was parked on the street when the search occurred and no evidence suggested it was incapable of movement.

## Probable Cause to Search a Person (page 346)
### NORTH CAROLINA COURT OF APPEALS (page 347)

**State v. Pigford**, ___ N.C. App. ___, 789 S.E.2d 857 (2016). An odor of marijuana emanating from inside a vehicle stopped at a checkpoint did not provide an officer with probable cause to conduct an immediate warrantless search of the driver. The defendant was driving the stopped vehicle, while a passenger sat in the front seat. The officer was unable to establish the exact location of the odor but determined that it was coming from inside the vehicle. Upon smelling the odor, the officer ordered the defendant out of the vehicle and searched him, finding cocaine and other items. On appeal the defendant argued that although the officer smelled marijuana emanating from the vehicle, there was no evidence the odor was attributable to the defendant personally. While the officer had probable cause to search the vehicle, that does not necessarily justify search of a passenger. The State offered no evidence that the marijuana odor was attributable to the defendant. The court held: the officer "may have had probable cause to search the vehicle, but he did not have probable cause to search defendant."

## Warrantless Entry with Exigent Circumstances to Search a Place for Evidence or Weapons (page 348)
### NORTH CAROLINA COURT OF APPEALS (page 349)

**State v. Marrero**, ___ N.C. App. ___, 789 S.E.2d 560 (2016). In this drug case, the trial court properly denied a motion to suppress where no illegal seizure of the defendant occurred during a knock and talk and where exigent circumstances justified the officers' warrantless entry into the defendant's home. The court rejected the defendant's argument that he was illegally seized during a knock and talk because he was coerced into opening the front door. The officers knocked on the front door a few times and stated that they were with the police only once during the two to three minutes it took the defendant to answer the door. There was no evidence that the defendant was aware of the officers' presence before he opened the door. Blue lights from nearby police cars were not visible to the defendant and no takedown lights were used. The officers did not try to open the door themselves or demand that it be opened. The court concluded: "[T]he officers did not act in a physically or verbally threatening manner" and no seizure of the defendant occurred during the knock and talk. Furthermore, exigent circumstances supported the officers' warrantless entry into the defendant's home. Officers arrived at the defendant's residence because of an informant's tip that armed suspects were going to rob a marijuana plantation located inside the house. When the officers arrived for the knock and talk, they did not know whether the robbery had occurred, was in progress, or was imminent. As soon as the defendant opened his door, an officer smelled a strong odor of marijuana. Based on that odor and the defendant's inability to understand English, the officers entered the defendant's home and secured it in preparation for obtaining a search warrant. On these facts, the trial court did not err in concluding that exigent circumstances warranted a protective sweep for officer safety and to ensure the defendant or others would not destroy evidence.

## Search and Seizure of Evidence from a Person's Body (page 358)

### NORTH CAROLINA SUPREME COURT (page 360)

**State v. Romano**, 369 N.C. 678 (2017). The court held, in this DWI case, that in light of the United States Supreme Court's decisions in *Birchfield v. North Dakota*, 579 U.S. ___, 136 S. Ct. 2160 (2016) (holding that the search incident to arrest doctrine does not justify the warrantless taking of a blood sample and that implied consent cannot be inferred when conditioned on criminal punishment), and *Missouri v. McNeely*, 569 U.S. 141 (2013) (holding that the natural dissipation of alcohol in the bloodstream does not constitute an exigency in every case sufficient to justify conducting a blood test without a warrant), and G.S. 20-16.2(b) (allowing blood to be drawn from an unconscious person without a warrant based on reasonable suspicion of impaired driving), the taking of the defendant's blood violated the Fourth Amendment. An officer, relying on G.S. 20-16.2(b), took possession of the defendant's blood from a treating nurse while the defendant was unconscious without first obtaining a warrant. The court rejected the State's implied consent argument, and stated:

> Here there is no dispute that the officer did not get a warrant and that there were no exigent circumstances. Regarding consent, the State's argument was based solely on [G.S.] 20-16.2(b) as a per se exception to the warrant requirement. To be sure, the implied-consent statute, as well as a person's decision to drive on public roads, are factors to consider when analyzing whether a suspect has consented to a blood draw, but the statute alone does not create a per se exception to the warrant requirement. The State did not present any other evidence of consent or argue that under the totality of the circumstances defendant consented to a blood draw. Therefore, the State did not carry its burden of proving voluntary consent. As such, the trial court correctly suppressed the blood evidence and any subsequent testing of the blood that was obtained without a warrant.

### NORTH CAROLINA COURT OF APPEALS (page 360)

**State v. Burris**, ___ N.C. App. ___, 799 S.E.2d 452 (2017). In this impaired driving case, the trial court properly denied the defendant's motion to suppress where exigent circumstances supported a warrantless blood draw. The defendant tested at .10 on a roadside test, was arrested at 2:48 a.m., and then was transported to the police department, where he arrived 18 minutes later. When the defendant refused to comply with further testing within two to three minutes after arriving at the police department, the detective decided to compel a blood test. The closest hospital was approximately four miles from the police department and eight miles from the magistrate's office. The detective read the defendant his rights regarding the blood draw at the hospital at 3:24 a.m. and waited for the defendant to finish making a phone call before starting the blood draw at 3:55 a.m. The detective testified that based on the information he had at the time, he thought the defendant was close to a blood alcohol level of .08. The detective further indicated that he thought it would have taken an additional hour to an hour and half to get a search warrant. The detective was the only officer on the scene and would have had to wait for another officer to arrive before he could travel to the magistrate to get the search warrant. The trial court's finding regarding the detective's reasonable belief that the delay would result in the dissipation of alcohol in the defendant's blood was supported by competent evidence. Thus, the trial court did not err in denying the defendant's motion to suppress the blood draw.

### Probation or Parole Officer's Search of Home (page 364)
**NORTH CAROLINA COURT OF APPEALS** (page 364)

*State v. Powell*, ___ N.C. App. ___, 800 S.E.2d 745 (2017). Because the State failed to meet its burden of demonstrating that a warrantless search was authorized by G.S. 15A-1343(b)(13), the trial court erred by denying the defendant's motion to suppress. The defendant was subject to the regular condition of probation under G.S. 15A-1343(b)(13). This provision requires that the probationer "[s]ubmit at reasonable times to warrantless searches by a probation officer of the probationer's person and of the probationer's vehicle and premises while the probationer is present, for purposes directly related to the probation supervision . . . ." Here, the search of the defendant's home occurred as part of an ongoing operation of a United States Marshal's Service task force. The court noted that while prior case law makes clear that the presence or participation of law enforcement officers does not, by itself, render a warrantless search under the statute unlawful, the State must meet its burden of satisfying the "purpose" element of the statute. The State failed to meet its burden here. To conclude otherwise would require the court to read the phrase "for purposes directly related to the probation supervision" out of the statute. The court emphasized that its opinion should not be read as diminishing the authority of probation officers to conduct warrantless searches of probationers' homes or to utilize the assistance of law enforcement officers in conducting such searches. Rather, it held that on the specific facts of this case the State failed to meet its burden of demonstrating that the search was authorized under the statute.

### Wiretapping, Eavesdropping, Digital Evidence, and Video Surveillance (page 365)
**NORTH CAROLINA COURT OF APPEALS** (page 366)

*State v. Forte*, ___ N.C. App. ___, 810 S.E.2d 339 (2018). The trial court issued an order authorizing law enforcement to access location information for the defendant's phone. The order was issued pursuant to the Stored Communications Act (SCA). The SCA requires only reasonable suspicion for issuance of an order for disclosure. The order in question was based on information provided by a known drug dealer informant, Oliver. The court found that there were "multiple indications of reliability" of Oliver's statements, including that he made substantial admissions against his penal interest. Also, Oliver provided a nickname, a general description of the defendant, background information from dealing with him previously, and current travel information regarding the defendant. Oliver spoke with the officer, and the two spoke more than once, adding to the reliability of his tip. These facts met the standard under the SCA. The court ruled that the defendant had not preserved any argument regarding whether the SCA's standard was unconstitutionally low.

## Protective Searches (page 371)
### Scope of Search Incident to Arrest (page 371)
*Generally* (page 371)
**NORTH CAROLINA COURT OF APPEALS** (page 374)

*State v. Fuller*, ___ N.C. App. ___, 809 S.E.2d 157 (2017). In this drug case, a search of the defendant's person was a proper search incident to arrest. An officer stopped the defendant's vehicle for driving with a revoked license and arrested the defendant. The officer then conducted a consent search of the vehicle that failed to locate any contraband, but a K-9 dog arrived and "hit" on the driver's seat cushion. When a second search uncovered no contraband or narcotics, the officer concluded that the narcotics must be on the defendant's person. The defendant was brought to the police department and was searched. The search involved lowering the defendant's pants and long johns to his knees. During the search the officer pulled out, but did not pull down, the defendant's underwear and observed the defendant's genitals and buttocks. Cocaine eventually was retrieved from a hidden area on the fly of the defendant's pants. The appellate court rejected the defendant's argument that the strip search could only have been conducted with probable cause and exigent circumstances, noting that standard applies only to roadside strip searches. Here, the search was conducted incident to the defendant's lawful arrest inside a private interview room at a police facility. Furthermore, the scope of the search was reasonable. It was limited to the area of the defendant's body and clothing that would have come in contact with the cushion of the driver's seat where the dog alerted, and the defendant was searched inside a private interview room at the police station with only the defendant and two officers present. The officers did not remove the defendant's clothing above the waist. They did not fully remove his undergarments, nor did they touch his genitals or any body cavity. The court thus concluded that the place, manner, justification, and scope of the search of the defendant's person were reasonable.

### *Arrest of an Occupant of a Vehicle* (page 375)
**NORTH CAROLINA COURT OF APPEALS** (page 376)

*State v. Martinez*, ___ N.C. App. ___, 795 S.E.2d 386 (2016). After the defendant's arrest for impaired driving, officers properly searched his vehicle as a search incident to arrest. Applying *Arizona v. Gant*, 556 U.S. 332 (2009), the court found that the officer had a reasonable basis to believe that evidence of impaired driving might be found in the vehicle. The defendant denied ownership, possession, and operation of the vehicle to the officer both verbally and by throwing the car keys under the vehicle. Based on the totality of the circumstances, including the strong odor of alcohol on the defendant, the defendant's efforts to hide the keys and refusal to unlock the vehicle, and the officer's training and experience with regard to impaired driving investigations, the trial court properly concluded that the officer reasonably believed the vehicle might have contained evidence of the offense. In the factual discussion, the court noted that the officer had testified that he had conducted between 20 and 30 impaired driving investigations, that at least 50 percent of those cases involved discovery of evidence associated with impaired driving inside the vehicle, such as open containers of alcohol, and that he had been trained to search a vehicle under these circumstances.

### *Protective Sweep of Premises* (page 377)
**NORTH CAROLINA COURT OF APPEALS** (page 377)

*State v. Smith*, ___ N.C. App. ___, 804 S.E.2d 235, *review allowed*, ___ N.C. ___, 807 S.E.2d 575 (2017). In this felon in possession of a firearm case, the trial court erred by denying the defendant's motion to suppress. Three officers entered the defendant's apartment to execute arrest warrants issued for misdemeanors. While two officers made the arrest, the third conducted a protective sweep of the defendant's apartment, leading to the discovery and seizure of a shotgun leaning against the wall in the entry of the defendant's bedroom. The bedroom door was open and the shotgun was visible, in plain view, from the hallway. The officer walked past the shotgun when checking the defendant's bedroom to confirm that no other occupants were present. After completing the sweep, the officer secured the shotgun "to have it in . . . control and also check to see if it was stolen." The officer located the serial number on the shotgun and called it into the police department, which reported that the gun was stolen. On review, the court determined that the protective sweep was proper, because the rooms in the apartment—including the bedroom where the shotgun was found—were areas immediately adjoining the place of arrest from which an attack could be immediately launched. However, over a dissent, the court held that the plain view doctrine could not justify seizure of the shotgun because the incriminating nature of the shotgun was not immediately apparent until after the officer manipulated the shotgun to reveal its serial number. The officers were executing arrest warrants for misdemeanor offenses and were not aware the defendant was a convicted felon. Manipulating the shotgun constituted a search, separate and apart from the lawful objective of the entry, and there was no legal basis for it. This case is currently before the North Carolina Supreme Court for its review.

## Frisk (page 379)
### *Generally* (page 379)
#### FEDERAL APPELLATE COURTS (page 379)

*United States v. Robinson*, 846 F.3d 694 (4th Cir. 2017) (en banc). "After receiving a[n anonymous] tip that a man in a parking lot well known for drug-trafficking activity had just loaded a firearm and then concealed it in his pocket before getting into a car as a passenger . . . police stopped the car after observing that its occupants were not wearing seatbelts. Reasonably believing that the . . . passenger . . . was armed, the police frisked him and uncovered the firearm, leading to his arrest for the possession of a firearm by a felon." The defendant moved to suppress, arguing that the officers lacked reasonable suspicion to believe that he was armed and dangerous, as they had no reason to believe that he was not a concealed carry permit holder. The Fourth Circuit disagreed, "concluding that an officer who makes a lawful traffic stop and who has a reasonable suspicion that one of the automobile's occupants is armed may frisk that individual for the officer's protection and the safety of everyone on the scene." The court determined that a risk of danger sufficient to justify a frisk arises "from the combination of a forced police encounter and the presence of a weapon," even if the weapon is possessed legally. Indeed, the court stated that "traffic stops alone are inherently dangerous for police officers." It also emphasized that whether a detainee is armed and dangerous does not require two separate inquiries; one who is "armed [is] therefore dangerous." The dissent would have rejected the idea that "armed" implies "dangerous" and argued that "there is no reason to think that a person carrying or concealing a weapon during a traffic stop—[when] fully sanctioned by state law—is anything but a law-abiding citizen who poses no threat to the authorities."

## Entering Premises for Public Safety Reasons (page 396)
#### NORTH CAROLINA COURT OF APPEALS (page 398)

*State v. Huddy*, ___ N.C. App. ___, 799 S.E.2d 650 (2017). An officer violated the defendant's Fourth Amendment rights by searching the curtilage of his home without a warrant. The officer saw a vehicle with its doors open at the back of a 150-yard driveway leading to the defendant's home. Concerned that the vehicle might be part of a break-in or home invasion, the officer drove down the driveway, ran the vehicle's tags, checked the windows and doors of the home for signs of forced entry, "cleared" the sides of the house, and then went through a closed gate in a chain-link fence enclosing the home's backyard and approached the storm door at the back of the house. As the officer approached the door, which was not visible from the street, he smelled marijuana, which led to the defendant's arrest for drug charges. The court determined that this was not a knock and talk because the officer went to a rear door not visible from the street and located behind a closed gate. Likewise, the community caretaking doctrine did not support the officer's actions because a vehicle's doors may stand ajar for many reasons that are not suspicious. "The presence of a vehicle in one's driveway with its doors open is not the sort of emergency that justifies the community caretaker exception." The court also noted that because the Fourth Amendment's protections "are at their very strongest within one's home," the public need justifying the community caretaking exception "must be particularly strong to justify a warrantless search of a home."

# Chapter 4

# Search Warrants, Administrative Inspection Warrants, and Nontestimonial Identification Orders

## Part I: Search Warrants (page 406)

### Introduction (page 406)
### Consequences of an Unlawful Search or Seizure (page 406)
### *Exclusionary Rules* (page 407)
#### North Carolina statutory exclusionary rule (page 408)
##### *Footnote 20* (page 408)

Add to footnote 20 the following citation: *Cf.* State v. Downey, ___ N.C. App. ___, 791 S.E.2d 257 (2016) (holding that the statutory exclusionary rule did not apply in a case in which the defendant claimed that the inventory was vague and inaccurate, as no evidence was seized as a result of any fault regarding the inventory).

### Description of the Property to Be Seized (page 413)

For a recent discussion of the requirement that the property to be seized be described with particularity, see Jeff Welty, *Particularly Describing the Evidence to Be Seized under a Search Warrant*, UNC Sch. of Gov't: N.C. Crim. L. Blog (Feb. 26, 2018), https://nccriminallaw.sog.unc.edu/particularly-describing-evidence-seized-search-warrant/.

### Obscene Materials, Including Child Pornography (page 418)

A recent case has resolved two legal questions concerning search warrants for child pornography. First, it is now clear that an application for a search warrant in a child pornography case does *not* need to include a copy of the image or images in question in order to establish probable cause.[1] Second, it is also now settled that when an image possessed by a suspect can be matched to a known image of child pornography through its SHA-1 or "hash" value, that is sufficient to provide probable cause.[2] When a SHA-1 match is not possible, officers will often seek search warrants based on verbal descriptions of images viewed by an officer or another witness; in such a case, the description may need to be rather detailed and explicit to be sufficient.[3]

---

1. State v. Gerard, ___ N.C. App. ___, ___, 790 S.E.2d 592, 599 (2016) (so holding, and stating that "[i]ncluding copies of the images themselves would further perpetuate the very harm the statutes regarding child pornography were intended to prevent," i.e., the dissemination of inappropriate images).

2. *Id.* (noting that SHA1 or SHA-1 is an "algorithm" that is "like a fingerprint," which may be used to identify digital files, and stating that "[u]sing the SHA1 information to identify the known images of child pornography eliminated the need to attach copies of the images to the affidavit").

3. For a summary of the case law regarding verbal descriptions of images, see Jeff Welty, *Probable Cause and Child Pornography*, UNC Sch. of Gov't: N.C. Crim. L. Blog (Feb. 12, 2018), https://nccriminallaw.sog.unc.edu/probable-cause-child-pornography/.

## Description of the Premises, the Person to Be Searched, or the Vehicle (page 419)

### The Premises (page 419)

#### Vehicles on the Premises (page 420)

In *State v. Lowe*,[4] the state supreme court ruled that a search warrant for a residence supported the search of a vehicle located within the curtilage of the home even though the vehicle (1) was not listed in the warrant and (2) did not belong to the occupant of the premises, as it was a rental vehicle in the possession of an overnight guest. The court stated that "[b]ecause the rental car was within the curtilage of the residence targeted by the search warrant, and because the rental car was a [place in which the object of the search, in this case drugs, could be located,] we conclude that the search of the rental car was authorized by the warrant."[5]

## Statement of Facts Showing Probable Cause to Search (page 423)

### Sources of Information to Establish Probable Cause (page 423)

#### Affiant's Use of Hearsay Information (page 425)

##### Information from confidential informants (page 426)

###### *Informant's credibility or the reliability of the informant's information* (page 427)

The evidence supporting an informant's reliability need not be overwhelming, as several recent cases illustrate. First, in *State v. Jackson*,[6] the court considered the following facts: Two officers, working on a drug investigation, "conducted a knock-and-talk at the home of a person they had never met."[7] The officers told the resident that she was facing potential criminal charges for possessing marijuana. The resident "agreed to provide information regarding where she obtained the marijuana."[8] She told the officers she had purchased the drugs from a named person at his residence two days earlier. She described the individual as well as his home and its location. Officers confirmed the accuracy of the suspect's name, description, and the location of his home. They also learned that the defendant had previously been charged with possessing marijuana. Relying on this information plus the fact that they had received several citizen complaints about possible marijuana dealing at the suspect's residence over the past year, the officers sought and obtained a search warrant for his home. When they executed the warrant, they found marijuana and indoor growing equipment.

The court determined that the search warrant was supported by sufficient probable cause. Although the informant did not have a "track record" of providing reliable information, the court found that she was sufficiently reliable. The court emphasized that the informant had a face-to-face communication with the officers, during which they could assess her demeanor; this significantly increased the likelihood that she would be held accountable for information that later proved to be false. The court also found it significant that the informant had first-hand knowledge of the information she conveyed, that the police independently corroborated certain information she provided, and that the information was recent. Finally, the court stated that the information provided by the informant was likely reliable because it was against her penal interest. (However, although she

---

4. 369 N.C. 360 (2016).

5. *Id.* at 367. For a longer discussion of *Lowe*, see Bob Farb, *North Carolina Supreme Court Upholds Search of Vehicle Located on Premises as Within Scope of Search Warrant*, UNC. Sch. of Gov't: N.C. Crim. L. Blog (Jan. 10, 2017), https://nccriminallaw.sog.unc.edu/north-carolina-supreme-court-upholds-search-vehicle-located-premises-within-scope-search-warrant/.

6. ___ N.C. App. ___, 791 S.E.2d 505, *aff'd*, 370 N.C. 337 (2017).

7. *Id.* at ___, 791 S.E.2d at 507.

8. *Id.*

admitted to criminal activity in purchasing and possessing marijuana, her motive in providing the information was apparently to reduce her criminal exposure rather than to come clean about her conduct.)[9]

The second recent case is *State v. Brody*.[10] It addresses how extensive an informant's track record must be before the informant may be deemed reliable. The case arose out of a drug investigation in Charlotte. An officer applied for a search warrant for the defendant's home, stating that the officer had received information from "a confidential and reliable informant"[11] that the defendant was dealing drugs from his residence. Specifically, the informant claimed to have been in the defendant's home over 30 times, including within the last 48 hours, and stated that he had seen evidence of drug dealing each time. Further, the affidavit indicated that the informant had "purchased cocaine from [the defendant] under the direct supervision of"[12] the officer, though the application did not detail the time, place, or circumstances of the purchase. The affidavit further stated that the officers had "known this informant for approximately two weeks"[13] and the informant had "provided information on other persons involved in drug trafficking . . . which we have investigated independently."[14] The controlled buy, of course, strongly supported probable cause, but the court also commented on the reliability of the informant, stating that "[t]he fact that the affidavit did not describe the precise outcomes of the previous tips . . . did not preclude a determination that the [informant] was reliable."[15] The court stated that "[a]lthough a general averment that an informant is 'reliable'—taken alone—might raise questions as to the basis for such an assertion,"[16] the fact that the detective also referenced receiving information from the informant in the past "allows for a reasonable inference that such information demonstrated the [confidential informant's] reliability."[17]

### Information from records (page 428)

A suspect's utility records may help establish probable cause by showing usage patterns consistent with criminal activity. For example, unusually high electricity consumption may be indicative of an indoor marijuana growing operation using artificial lights. However, for this evidence to be meaningful, officers should provide context: "The weight given to power records increases when meaningful comparisons are made between a suspect's current electricity consumption and prior consumption, or between a suspect's consumption and that of nearby, similar properties."[18]

---

9. For more information about *Jackson*, see Jeff Welty, *Drug Users, Drug Sellers, and Probable Cause*, UNC SCH. OF GOV'T: N.C. CRIM. L. BLOG (Oct. 11, 2016), https://nccriminallaw.sog.unc.edu/drug-users-drug-sellers-probable-cause/.

10. ___ N.C. App. ___, 796 S.E.2d 384 (2017).

11. *Id.* at ___, 796 S.E.2d at 387.

12. *Id.*

13. *Id.*

14. *Id.*

15. *Id.* at ___, 796 S.E.2d at 389.

16. State v. Brody, ___ N.C. App. ___, ___, 796 S.E.2d 384, 389 (2017).

17. *Id.*

18. State v. Benters, 367 N.C. 660, 670 (2014) (finding no probable cause despite an officer's statement that "the kilowatt usage hours [at the target residence] are indicative of a marijuana grow operation based on the extreme high and low kilowatt usage" because "the absence of any comparative analysis severely limits the potentially significant value of defendant's utility records").

### The Connection between a Crime, the Evidence to Be Seized, and the Place to Be Searched (page 430)

Several recent cases have addressed whether certain facts, clearly sufficient to establish probable cause that a crime had been committed, provided a sufficient nexus to a premises to support the search of that location. *State v. Allman*[19] is a case in which the North Carolina Supreme Court ultimately found that the facts showed a connection between a crime and the suspects' residence sufficient to support a search of the home. A deputy stopped and searched a car occupied by two half-brothers, finding marijuana and $1,600 in cash. Both occupants had prior drug arrests or convictions. One of them told the deputy that they lived together at an address in Castle Hayne, but when an officer later went to the residence, the men's mother answered the door and said they lived at a different residence in Wilmington.

The deputy obtained a search warrant for the Wilmington address based on (1) the vehicle's contents, (2) the men's history, (3) the officer's experience that drug dealers often keep evidence of drug dealing at their homes, and (4) the false statement regarding the men's address. The case eventually reached the state supreme court, which ruled that there was probable cause to support the search warrant. *Allman* does not go so far as to hold that evidence that a person is involved in drug activity will *always* allow a search of the person's residence. However, in this case, the facts cited above, especially the officer's experience and the false statement about where the men lived, were sufficient to support the issuance of the warrant.[20]

On the other hand, *State v. Lewis*[21] is an example of a case in which officers did *not* present a sufficient nexus to a premises. Officers investigated a series of armed robberies. They determined that the robberies had been committed by Robert Lewis, and that he had used a Kia Optima or a Nissan Titan in each crime. An officer determined Lewis lived at 7085 Laurinburg Road, went there, and saw an Optima and a Titan parked at the home. When Lewis came out of the residence, the officer arrested him. Another officer then applied for a search warrant for the vehicles and the residence. The application tied Lewis to the robberies and the robberies to the vehicles. As to the residence, however, the application stated only that the officers had "arrested Lewis at a residence located at 7085 Laurinburg Road"[22]—it did not indicate that Lewis lived at the residence, even though the officers knew he did. A magistrate issued the warrant, but the court of appeals eventually ruled that the warrant was not supported by probable cause with respect to the residence. It reasoned that "from the information in the affidavit, 7085 Laurinburg Road could have been someone else's home with no connection to Lewis at all. That Lewis visited that location, without some indication that he may have stowed incriminating evidence there, is not enough to justify a search of the home."[23] At this writing, *Lewis* has been stayed by the state supreme court.[24]

---

19. 369 N.C. 292 (2016).

20. For further discussion of *Allman*, see Bob Farb, *North Carolina Supreme Court Upholds a Magistrate's Finding of Probable Cause to Issue Search Warrant to Search Home for Drugs*, UNC Sch. of Gov't: N.C. Crim. L. Blog (Jan. 24, 2017), https://nccriminallaw.sog.unc.edu/north-carolina-supreme-court-upholds-magistrates-finding-probable-cause-issue-search-warrant-search-home-drugs/.

21. ___ N.C. App. ___, ___ S.E.2d ___, 2018 WL 2011955 (May 1, 2018), *temp. stay allowed,* ___ N.C. ___, 812 S.E.2d 856 (May 17, 2018).

22. *Id.* at ___, ___ S.E.2d at ___.

23. *Id.* at ___, ___ S.E.2d at ___. For additional discussion of *Lewis*, see Jeff Welty, *Failure to Include Known Facts in a Search Warrant Application Can Undermine Probable Cause*, UNC Sch. of Gov't: N.C. Crim. L. Blog (May 3, 2018), https://nccriminallaw.sog.unc.edu/failure-to-include-known-facts-in-a-search-warrant-application-can-undermine-probable-cause/.

24. A related issue is the extent to which probable cause to believe that a person committed a crime provides probable cause to search the person's cell phone for evidence of the crime. For a discussion of that issue, see Jeff Welty, *Probable Cause and Search Warrants for Cell Phones*, UNC Sch. of Gov't: N.C. Crim. L. Blog (Oct. 3, 2016), https://nccriminallaw.sog.unc.edu/probable-cause-search-warrants-cell-phones/.

## Execution and Return of the Search Warrant (page 437)
### Scope of the Search (page 440)
#### *Vehicles on the Premises* (page 442)

In *State v. Lowe*,[25] the state supreme court ruled that a search warrant for a residence supported the search of a vehicle located within the curtilage of the home even though the vehicle (1) was not listed in the warrant and (2) did not belong to the occupant of the premises, as it was a rental vehicle in the possession of an overnight guest. The court stated that "[b]ecause the rental car was within the curtilage of the residence targeted by the search warrant, and because the rental car was a [place in which the object of the search, in this case drugs, could be located,] we conclude that the search of the rental car was authorized by the warrant."[26]

# Part II. Administrative Inspection Warrants (page 448)

## Authority for Issuing Administrative Inspection Warrants (page 448)

In the 2016 legislative session, the General Assembly made minor revisions to the city (Chapter 160A, Section 424, of the North Carolina General Statutes (hereinafter G.S.)) and county (G.S. 153A-364) inspection statutes discussed in the main text.[27] The revisions do not affect the discussion of legal principles in the main text.

# Part III. Nontestimonial Identification Orders (page 459)

## Application for the Order and Issuance of the Order; Adult and Juvenile Suspect Forms (page 461)

The main text states that the adult forms should be used for "a person who is charged with a crime after his or her 16th birthday," as well as for a juvenile who has been charged as an adult or who has been transferred to adult court. Footnote 275 explains that age 16 is the cutoff because G.S. 7B-2103 governs nontestimonial identification orders for juveniles "alleged to be delinquent," which under current law means juveniles under age 16. However, the Juvenile Justice Reinvestment Act, S.L. 2017-57, Section 16D.4., raises the age of juvenile jurisdiction to 18 in most cases, effective December 1, 2019. Therefore, after that date, the adult forms should be used only for a person age 18 and over or for a juvenile who has been charged as an adult or who has been transferred to adult court.

---

25. 369 N.C. 360 (2016).

26. *Id.* at 367. For a longer discussion of *Lowe*, see Bob Farb, *North Carolina Supreme Court Upholds Search of Vehicle Located on Premises as Within Scope of Search Warrant*, UNC SCH. OF GOV'T: N.C. CRIM. L. BLOG (Jan. 10, 2017), https://nccriminallaw.sog.unc.edu/north-carolina-supreme-court-upholds-search-vehicle-located-premises-within-scope-search-warrant/.

27. *See* S.L. 2016-122.

## Juveniles and Nontestimonial Identification Procedures (page 464)

### Juvenile's Age (page 465)

The Juvenile Justice Reinvestment Act, S.L. 2017-57, Section 16D.4., raises the age of juvenile jurisdiction to 18 in most cases, effective December 1, 2019. As described immediately above, this appears to render the juvenile nontestimonial identification procedures, rather than the adult procedures, relevant for 16- and 17-year-old suspects.

# Chapter 4 Appendix: Case Summaries

# I. Search Warrants (page 475)

## Probable Cause (page 475)
### Generally (page 475)
#### NORTH CAROLINA SUPREME COURT (page 475)

*State v. Lowe*, 369 N.C. 360 (2016). A search warrant authorizing a search of the premises where the defendant was arrested was supported by probable cause. The affidavit stated that officers received an anonymous tip that Michael Turner was selling, using, and storing narcotics at his house; that Turner had a history of drug-related arrests; and that a detective discovered marijuana residue in the trash from Turner's residence, along with correspondence addressed to Turner. Under the totality of the circumstances, there was probable cause to search the home for controlled substances.

#### NORTH CAROLINA COURT OF APPEALS (page 479)

*State v. Lenoir*, ___ N.C. App. ___, ___ S.E.2d ___, 2018 WL 2638469 (June 5, 2018), *temp. stay allowed,* ___ N.C. App. ___, ___ S.E.2d ___ (June 25, 2018). In this possession of a firearm by a felon case, the court held that the application contained insufficient details to support issuance of the search warrant. When officers went to the defendant's home to conduct a knock and talk, the defendant's brother answered the door and invited them in. An officer asked if anyone else was present and the brother said he was alone but gave consent for an officer to check a back bedroom. In the bedroom the officer saw a woman lying on a bed and a "glass smoke pipe" on a dresser. The officer applied for and was issued a search warrant for the residence. A search of the home revealed a shotgun in the bedroom. After the defendant admitted he owned the gun, he was charged with possession of a firearm by a felon. On review, the court observed that the affidavit stated that the officer saw a "smoke pipe used for methamphetamine" in the bedroom. The application did not mention the officer's training and experience, nor did the officer provide information explaining the basis for his belief that the pipe was being used to smoke methamphetamine as opposed to tobacco. The affidavit did not explain how the officer was qualified to distinguish between a pipe used for lawful versus unlawful purposes. And it did not purport to describe in any detail the appearance of the pipe or contain any indication as to whether it appeared to have been recently used. It further lacked any indication that information had been received connecting the defendant or his home to drugs. The court stated that "a pipe—standing alone—is neither contraband nor evidence of a crime." Because the affidavit was insufficient to establish probable cause for issuance of the warrant, the trial court erred in denying the defendant's motion to suppress. At this writing, the state supreme court has entered a temporary stay of this ruling.

### Timeliness or Staleness of Information (page 484)
#### NORTH CAROLINA COURT OF APPEALS (page 484)

*State v. Teague*, ___ N.C. App. ___, ___ S.E.2d ___, 2018 WL 2627078 (June 5, 2018). In this drug case, the court held that the application provided sufficient probable cause to support the issuance of a search warrant for the defendant's residence. The affidavit indicated that after the officer received an anonymous tip that drugs were being sold at the residence, he conducted a "refuse investigation" at the premises, finding evidence of drug activity in the trash. The defendant asserted that this information was stale and could not properly support issuance of the warrant. The court noted that although the affidavit did not state when or over what period of time the tipster observed criminal activity at the residence, when the tipster relayed the information to the police, or the exact date the officer conducted the refuse search, the affidavit was based on more than just this information. Specifically, it included details regarding database searches indicating that the defendant had a waste and water utility account at the residence, that the defendant lived at the residence, that the officer was familiar with the residence and the defendant from his previous assignment as a patrol officer, and that the defendant had prior drug charges. To the extent that the information in the anonymous tip was stale, it was later corroborated by the refuse search in which the officer found evidence consistent with the manufacturing of butane hash oil. The affidavit stated that the officer conducted the refuse investigation on Thursday, "regular refuse day." A common-sense reading of the affidavit would indicate that this referred to the most recent Thursday, the date the affidavit was completed. Thus, even if the anonymous tip was so stale as to be unreliable, the marijuana-related items obtained from the refuse search, the defendant's criminal history, and the database searches linking the defendant to the residence provided a substantial basis upon which the magistrate could determine that probable cause existed.

**State v. Howard**, ___ N.C. App. ___, ___ S.E.2d ___, 2018 WL 2627023 (June 5, 2018). In this felony counterfeit trademarked goods case, the court held that a search warrant was supported by probable cause. An officer obtained a search warrant to search the residence and vehicles at 13606 Coram Place in Charlotte, North Carolina. The officer had 26 years of law enforcement experience and had investigated thousands of counterfeit merchandise cases. The application stated that in May 2013, another officer informed the applicant that the defendant was found in possession of possible counterfeit items and was charged with violating the peddlers' license ordinance. The items seized were later confirmed to be counterfeit. In October 2013, as part of a compliance check/counterfeit merchandise interdiction operation at a shipping hub in Charlotte, the officer intercepted two packages from a known counterfeit merchandise distributor in China, addressed to the defendant at the residence in question. The boxes contained counterfeit items. The officer attempted a controlled delivery of the packages at the residence but no one was home. Two other packages previously delivered by the shipper were on the porch. The officer contacted the defendant, who agreed to meet with him and bring the two packages. The defendant consented to a search of the packages and they were found to contain counterfeit merchandise. The defendant said she did not realize the merchandise was counterfeit and voluntarily surrendered all of the merchandise. She was issued a warning. In November 2013, while the officer was working as part of a compliance check at a football game, the defendant was found selling counterfeit items. The defendant was charged with felony criminal use of counterfeit trademark and pled guilty to the lesser misdemeanor charge. During another compliance check outside of the Charlotte Convention Center in May 2015, the officer found a booth with a large display of counterfeit items. The booth was unmanned but business cards listed the owner as "Tammy." The officer verified that the address listed in the search warrant was the residence of the defendant, Tammy Renee Howard. During a search of the premises pursuant to the warrant, hundreds of counterfeit items with an approximate retail value of $2 million were seized. On appeal the defendant asserted that the affidavit contained insufficient evidence to support a reasonable belief that evidence of counterfeit items would be found at the premises. The affidavit included evidence of the delivery of counterfeit merchandise to the premises, evidence that the defendant continued to conduct her illegal business after warnings and arrests, and evidence that the officer confirmed the defendant resided at the premises. The defendant also argued that the evidence in the affidavit was stale, noting that the only evidence linking the premises with criminal activity allegedly took place in October 2013, some 20 months prior to the issuance of the warrant. However, the evidence showed that the defendant was conducting a business involving counterfeit goods over a number of years at numerous locations and involving the need to acquire counterfeit merchandise from China. For all these reasons, the defendant's motion to suppress was properly denied.

# Information from a Confidential Informant (page 486)

## *Informant's Credibility or the Reliability of the Informant's Information* (page 486)

### NORTH CAROLINA SUPREME COURT (page 486)

*State v. Jackson*, 370 N.C. 337 (2017). On appeal from a decision of a divided panel of the court of appeals, ___ N.C. App. ___, 791 S.E.2d 505 (2016), the state supreme court affirmed in a per curiam opinion. Over a dissent, the court of appeals had held that the search warrant was supported by sufficient probable cause. At issue was the reliability of information provided by a confidential informant. Applying the totality of the circumstances test, and although the informant did not have a "track record" of providing reliable information, the court found that the informant was sufficiently reliable. The court noted that the information provided by the informant was against her penal interest because, in the course of providing information about her drug supplier, she acknowledged purchasing and possessing marijuana. The court further observed that the informant had a face-to-face communication with the officer, during which he could assess her demeanor; the face-to-face conversation significantly increased the likelihood the informant would be held accountable for a tip that later proved to be false; the informant had first-hand knowledge of the information she conveyed; the police independently corroborated certain information she provided regarding the name and address of the supplier; and the information was not stale, as the informant was describing transactions from just two days before.

### NORTH CAROLINA COURT OF APPEALS (page 486)

*State v. McPhaul*, ___ N.C. App. ___, 808 S.E.2d 294 (2017), *review allowed*, ___ N.C. ___, 812 S.E.2d 847 (2018). In this attempted murder and robbery case, a search warrant was supported by probable cause. On appeal, the defendant argued that the warrant lacked probable cause because a statement by a confidential informant provided the only basis to believe evidence might be found at the premises in question and the supporting affidavit failed to establish the informant's reliability. The court disagreed. The detective's affidavit detailed a meeting between an officer and the confidential informant in which the informant stated that he witnessed described individuals running from the crime scene and that one of them entered the premises in question. The informant's statement corroborated significant matters previously known to the police department, including the general time and location of the offenses, the victim's physical description of his assailants, and the suspect's possession of items similar in appearance to those stolen from the victim. The affidavit therefore demonstrated the informant's reliability. The state supreme court has agreed to review this case.

*State v. Brody*, ___ N.C. App. ___, 796 S.E.2d 384 (2017). In this drug case, a search warrant application relying principally upon information obtained from a confidential informant was sufficient to support a magistrate's finding of probable cause and a subsequent search of the defendant's home. The court rejected the defendant's argument that the affidavit failed to show that the confidential informant was reliable and that drugs were likely to be found in the home. The affidavit stated that investigators had known the confidential informant for two weeks, that the informant had previously provided them with information regarding other people involved in drug trafficking, and that the detective considered the informant reliable. The confidential informant had demonstrated to the detective that he was familiar with drug pricing and with how controlled substances are packaged and sold for distribution. Moreover, the informant had previously arranged and negotiated the purchase of and purchased cocaine from the defendant under the detective's direct supervision, though the application did not extensively detail these transactions. Additionally, the confidential informant told the detective that he had visited the defendant's home approximately 30 times, including within 48 hours before the affidavit was prepared, and saw the defendant possessing and selling cocaine each time. The court noted: "The fact that the affidavit did not describe the precise outcomes of the previous tips from the [informant] did not preclude a determination that the [informant] was reliable." It added: "[A]lthough a general averment that an informant is 'reliable'—taken alone—might raise questions as to the basis for such an assertion," the fact that the detective also specifically stated that investigators had received information from the informant in the past "allows for a reasonable inference that such information demonstrated the [confidential informant's] reliability." Moreover, the detective had further opportunity to gauge his reliability when the informant arranged and negotiated the purchase of and purchased cocaine from the defendant under the detective's supervision.

**State v. Kirkman**, ___ N.C. App. ___, 795 S.E.2d 379 (2016). In this drug case, a search warrant was properly supported by probable cause. At issue was whether a confidential informant was sufficiently reliable to support a finding of probable cause. The affidavit noted that the confidential informant was familiar with the appearance of illegal narcotics and that all previous information the informant provided had proven to be truthful and accurate. This information was sufficient to establish the confidential informant's reliability.

## Probable Cause for Premises to Be Searched (page 487)

### NORTH CAROLINA SUPREME COURT (page 487)

**State v. Allman**, 369 N.C. 292 (2016). Reversing the court of appeals, the court held that a magistrate had a substantial basis to find that probable cause existed to issue a search warrant. The affidavit stated that an officer stopped a car driven by Jeremy Black. Black's half-brother Sean Whitehead was a passenger. After a K-9 alerted on the car, a search found 8.1 ounces of marijuana and $1,600 in cash. Both individuals had previously been charged on several occasions with drug crimes. Whitehead maintained that the two lived at Twin Oaks Drive in Castle Hayne. The officer went to that address and found that although neither individual lived there, their mother did. The mother informed the officer that the men lived at 4844 Acres Drive in Wilmington and had not lived at Twin Oaks Drive for years. Another officer went to the Acres Drive premises and determined that its description matched that given by the mother and that a truck outside the house was registered to Black. The officer had experience with drug investigations and, based on his training and experience, knew that drug dealers typically keep evidence of drug dealing at their homes. Supported by the affidavit, the officer applied for and received a search warrant to search the Acres Drive home. Drugs and paraphernalia were found. On review, the court found that the warrant was properly issued. Based on the quantity of marijuana and the amount of cash found in the car, the fact that the marijuana appeared to be packaged for sale, and Whitehead's and Black's criminal histories, the magistrate reasonably inferred that the brothers were drug dealers. Based on the mother's statement that the two lived at the Acres Drive premises, the fact that her description of that home matched its actual appearance, and the fact that one of the trucks there was registered to Black, the magistrate reasonably inferred that the two lived there. And based on the insight from the officer's training and experience that evidence of drug dealing was likely to be found at their home and the fact that Whitehead lied about where the two lived, the magistrate reasonably inferred there could be evidence of drug dealing at the Acres Drive premises. Although nothing in the affidavit directly connected the defendant's home with evidence of drug dealing, federal circuit courts have held that a suspect drug dealer's lie about his address in combination with other evidence of drug dealing can give rise to probable cause to search the suspect's home. Thus, under the totality of the circumstances, there was probable cause to support the search warrant.

### NORTH CAROLINA COURT OF APPEALS (page 488)

**State v. Howard**, ___ N.C. App. ___, ___ S.E.2d ___, 2018 WL 2627023 (June 5, 2018). In this felony counterfeit trademarked goods case, the court held that a search warrant was supported by probable cause. An officer obtained a search warrant to search the residence and vehicles at 13606 Coram Place in Charlotte, North Carolina. The officer had 26 years of law enforcement experience and had investigated thousands of counterfeit merchandise cases. The application stated that in May 2013, another officer informed the applicant that the defendant was found in possession of possible counterfeit items and was charged with violating the peddlers' license ordinance. The items seized were later confirmed to be counterfeit. In October 2013, as part of a compliance check/counterfeit merchandise interdiction operation at a shipping hub in Charlotte, the officer intercepted two packages from a known counterfeit merchandise distributor in China, addressed to the defendant at the residence in question. The boxes contained counterfeit items. The officer attempted a controlled delivery of the packages at the residence but no one was home. Two other packages previously delivered by the shipper were on the porch. The officer contacted the defendant, who agreed to meet with him and bring the two packages. The defendant consented to a search of the packages and they were found to contain counterfeit merchandise. The defendant said she did not realize the merchandise was counterfeit and voluntarily surrendered all of the merchandise. She was issued a warning. In November 2013, while the officer was working as part of a compliance check at a football game, the defendant was found selling counterfeit items. The defendant was charged with felony criminal use of counterfeit trademark and pled guilty to the lesser misdemeanor charge. During another compliance check outside of the Charlotte Convention Center in May 2015 the officer found a booth with a large display of counterfeit items. The booth was unmanned but business cards listed the owner as "Tammy." The officer verified that the address listed in the search warrant was the residence of the defendant, Tammy Renee Howard. During a search of the premises pursuant to the warrant, hundreds of counterfeit items with an approximate retail value of $2 million were seized. On appeal the defendant asserted that the affidavit contained insufficient evidence to support a reasonable belief that evidence of counterfeit items would be found at the premises. The affidavit included evidence of the delivery of counterfeit merchandise to the premises, evidence that the defendant continued to conduct her illegal business after warnings and arrests, and evidence that the officer confirmed the defendant resided at the premises. The defendant also argued that the evidence in the affidavit was stale, noting that the only evidence linking the premises with criminal activity allegedly took place in October 2013, some 20 months prior to the issuance of the warrant. However, the evidence showed that the defendant was conducting a business involving counterfeit goods over a number of years at numerous locations and involving the need to acquire counterfeit merchandise from China. For all these reasons, the defendant's motion to suppress was properly denied.

**State v. Lewis**, ___ N.C. App. ___, ___ S.E.2d ___, 2018 WL 2011955 (May 1, 2018), *temp. stay allowed*, ___ N.C. ___, 812 S.E.2d 856 (May 17, 2018). In this robbery and kidnapping case, the court held that although the warrant application and accompanying affidavit contained sufficient information to establish probable cause to search two vehicles, it did not contain sufficient information to establish probable cause to search a residence where the defendant was arrested. Deputies were investigating a string of armed robberies of dollar stores. A local police department contacted them about a similar robbery that had just taken place. The police stated that they had seen a man they knew as Robert Lewis fleeing the scene. A deputy then "drove to Lewis's address, 7085 Laurinburg Road," and saw a Kia Optima and a Nissan Titan parked there. Witnesses had reported that the robber had used a Kia Optima and a Nissan Titan in the robberies. The deputy parked and watched the house until he saw "a man matching Lewis's description walk from the house out to the mailbox and take mail out." The officer approached the man, who identified himself as Robert Lewis. The officer arrested Lewis on a warrant the police department had obtained. The officer also determined that Lewis lived at the premises. Officers then obtained a search warrant to search the premises, including the two vehicles. Although the defendant's motion to suppress was denied, the defendant prevailed on appeal. The court began by finding that the warrant application contained sufficient facts to establish probable cause to search the vehicles. But it went on to agree with the defendant that the affidavit did not establish probable cause to search the home. Although the defendant resided at the home, the affidavit did not state that. The only information in the affidavit tying the defendant to the home was a statement that officers observed a dark blue Nissan Titan at the residence while arresting the defendant. The court concluded: "[T]his statement is sufficient to establish that [the defendant] was found at that location; but it does not follow from that statement that [the defendant] also must reside at that location." "Indeed," it continued, "from the information in the affidavit, [the home] could have been someone else's home with no connection to [the defendant] at all." It concluded: "That [the defendant] visited that location, without some indication that he may have stowed incriminating evidence there, is not enough to justify a search of the home." At this writing, the state supreme court has entered a temporary stay of this ruling.

*State v. Frederick*, ___ N.C. App. ___, ___ S.E.2d ___, 2018 WL 1801542 (Apr. 17, 2018). A detective sought a search warrant for the defendant's home. The affidavit in support of the application stated a "confidential source" had recently given the officer "information . . . regarding a [drug] dealer." The detective considered the source reliable, as he had provided accurate information in the past. The detective and the source attempted to corroborate the information by conducting two controlled buys in the week before the application was submitted. In both cases, the informant met with a "middle man," who was apparently unknown to the detective, and took him to the suspect's home. Officers watched the middleman enter the home and exit a few minutes later. The informant dropped the middleman off at his residence and then met with the detective. Each time, the informant had no drugs at the outset, and had drugs at the end of the expedition. A magistrate issued a search warrant based on these transactions, and the reviewing court ruled that this was proper.

*State v. Worley*, ___ N.C. App. ___, 803 S.E.2d 412 (2017). The trial court properly denied the defendant's motion to suppress evidence seized pursuant to search warrants for his rental cabin and truck. The defendant argued that the search warrant application established no nexus between the cabin and the criminal activity—the theft of goods during a breaking and entering of a horse trailer. The court found, however, "that under the totality of the circumstances, the accumulation of reasonable inferences drawn from information contained within the affidavit sufficiently linked the criminal activity to defendant's cabin." Among other things, the affidavit established that when one of the property owners hired the defendant to work at their farm, several tools and pieces of equipment went missing and were never recovered; immediately before the defendant moved out of state, someone broke into their daughter's car and stole property; the defendant rented a cabin close to their property around the same time as the reported breaking and entering and larceny; and the defendant had prior convictions for first-degree burglary and felony larceny. Based on this and other evidence discussed in detail in the court's opinion, the affidavit established a sufficient nexus between the criminal activity and the defendant's cabin.

*State v. Parson*, ___ N.C. App. ___, 791 S.E.2d 528 (2016). The trial court erred by denying the defendant's motion to suppress evidence seized pursuant to a search warrant. The court found that the application for the search warrant insufficiently connected the address in question to the objects sought. It noted that none of the allegations in the affidavit specifically referred to the address in question and none established the required nexus between the objects sought (evidence of manufacturing methamphetamine) and the place to be searched. The court further stated that the defendant's refusal of an officer's request to search the property cannot establish probable cause to search.

## Search Warrants for Obscene Materials (page 497)

**NORTH CAROLINA COURT OF APPEALS** (page 498)

*State v. Gerard*, ___ N.C. App. ___, 790 S.E.2d 592 (2016). In this sexual exploitation of a minor case, the information contained in an officer's affidavit was sufficient to provide probable cause for issuance of a search warrant for child pornography. An officer and certified computer forensic examiner identified images possessed by the defendant as child pornography through the use of an SHA1 algorithm or hash value, which the court noted is an "algorithm" that is "like a fingerprint" that may be used to identify digital files. Although less detailed than the officer's testimony at the hearing, the affidavit described technical detail regarding law enforcement methods and software used to identify and track transmissions of child pornography over the Internet. The court rejected the defendant's argument that the affidavit's identification of alleged pornographic images as known child pornography based upon computer information was insufficient and that the pictures themselves must be provided with the affidavit.

## Executing a Search Warrant (page 498)

### Service of a Search Warrant and Completion of an Inventory (page 506)

**NORTH CAROLINA COURT OF APPEALS** (page 506)

*State v. Downey*, ___ N.C. App. ___, 791 S.E.2d 257 (2016). In this drug case, the court rejected the defendant's argument that the trial court erred by denying his motion to suppress evidence collected from his residence on the grounds that the inventory list prepared by the detective was unlawfully vague and inaccurate in describing the items seized. The defendant argued that the evidence gathered from his residence was obtained in substantial violation of G.S. 15A-254, which requires an officer executing a search warrant to write and sign a receipt itemizing the items taken. However, in order for suppression to be warranted for a substantial violation of Chapter 15A, G.S. 15A-974 requires that the evidence be obtained as a result of an officer's unlawful conduct and that it would not have been obtained but for the unlawful conduct. Here, citing prior case law, the court held, in part, that because the evidence was seized before the inventory required by the statute had to be prepared, the defendant failed to show that the evidence would not have been obtained but for the alleged violations of G.S. 15A-254. The court held that G.S. 15A-254 "applies only after evidence has been obtained and does not implicate the right to be free from unreasonable search and seizure. In turn, because evidence cannot be obtained 'as a result of' a violation of [G.S.] 15A-254, [G.S.] 15A-974(a)(2) is inapplicable to either alleged or actual [G.S.] 15A-254 violations."

## Scope of the Search and Seizure with a Search Warrant (page 508)

### Searching Vehicles Not Named in the Warrant (page 511)

**NORTH CAROLINA SUPREME COURT** (page 511)

*State v. Lowe*, 369 N.C. 360 (2016). The court held that a search of a vehicle located within the curtilage of a residence was within the scope of a search warrant for the home even though the vehicle in question was a rental car in the possession of the defendant, an overnight guest at the house. The court stated that if a search warrant validly describes the premises to be searched, a car on the premises may be searched even though the warrant contains no description of the car. In departing from this general rule, the court of appeals had held that the search of the car was invalid because the officers knew that the vehicle in question did not belong to the suspect in the drug investigation. Noting that the record was unclear as to what the officers knew about ownership and control of the vehicle, the state supreme court concluded: "[R]egardless of whether the officers knew the car was a rental, we hold that the search was within the scope of the warrant."

# IV. Suppression Motions and Hearings; Exclusionary Rules (page 534)

## General Exclusionary Rules (page 550)

### Derivative Evidence: Fruit of the Poisonous Tree (page 551)

**NORTH CAROLINA COURT OF APPEALS** (page 552)

*State v. Burwell*, ___ N.C. App. ___, 808 S.E.2d 583 (2017). In an assault on a law enforcement officer inflicting serious bodily injury case, the trial court did not err by denying the defendant's motion to suppress evidence of his attack on the officer, alleged by the defendant to be proper resistance to an unlawful arrest. The court concluded: "Even if a police officer's conduct violates a defendant's Fourth Amendment rights, evidence of an attack on an officer is not fruit of a poisonous tree subject to suppression." It elaborated:

"The doctrine of the fruit of the poisonous tree is a specific application of the exclusionary rule[,]" providing for the suppression of "all evidence obtained as a result of illegal police conduct." However, this doctrine does not permit evidence of attacks on police officers to be excluded, even "where those attacks occur while the officers are engaging in conduct that violates a defendant's Fourth Amendment rights." Thus, where a defendant argues an initial stop or subsequent arrest violated "his Fourth Amendment rights, the evidence of his crimes against the officers would not be considered excludable 'fruits' pursuant to the doctrine." (citations omitted).

Here, the defendant sought suppression of evidence of an attack on a police officer. The court concluded: "Defendant seeks the suppression of evidence of an attack on a police officer. Since evidence of an attack on a police officer cannot be suppressed as a fruit of the poisonous tree, the evidence Defendant sought to suppress cannot be suppressed as a matter of law."

***State v. Hester***, ___ N.C. App. ___, 803 S.E.2d 8 (2017). The court held, over a dissent, that even if the initial stop was not supported by reasonable suspicion, the trial court properly denied the defendant's motion to suppress where the evidence sought to be suppressed—a stolen handgun—was obtained after the defendant committed a separate crime: pointing a loaded gun at the deputy and pulling the trigger. The evidence at issue was admissible under the attenuation doctrine, which holds that evidence is admissible when the connection between the unconstitutional police conduct and the evidence is remote or has been interrupted by some intervening circumstance, so that the interest protected by the constitutional guarantee that has been violated would not be served by suppression. Here, the defendant's commission of a crime broke any causal chain between the presumably unlawful stop and the discovery of the stolen handgun.

# Chapter 5

# Interrogation and Confessions, Lineups and Other Identification Procedures, and Undercover Officers and Informants

## Part I. Interrogation and Confessions (page 565)

### Unconstitutional Seizure and the Resulting Statement (page 566)

One specific scenario that arises with some frequency involves an officer's decision to question a motorist, stopped for a traffic violation, about the motorist's suspected involvement in criminal activity. The extent to which an officer may do so is addressed in a new School of Government publication, Shea Riggsbee Denning, Christopher Tyner & Jeff Welty, *Pulled Over: The Law of Traffic Stops and Offenses in North Carolina* 60–61 (UNC School of Government, 2017).

### Recording Custodial Interrogations at a Place of Detention (page 567)

The main text notes on page 567 that Section 211 of Chapter 15A of the North Carolina General Statutes (hereinafter G.S.) requires the recording of "all custodial interrogations of juveniles in criminal investigations conducted at any place of detention," and explains in footnote 13 the uncertainty regarding whether "juvenile" for this purpose means a person under age 16 (the age of juvenile jurisdiction under current law) or a person under age 18 (the general legal meaning of the term). The Juvenile Justice Reinvestment Act, commonly known as the "raise the age" law, raises the age of juvenile jurisdiction to 18 for most purposes and eliminates this conflict. Once the raise the age law takes effect on December 1, 2019, the better reading of the term "juvenile" in G.S. 15A-211 clearly will be a person under age 18.[1]

### Voluntariness of the Defendant's Statement (page 569)

A recent case applying and illustrating some of the principles discussed in the main text is *State v. Johnson*.[2] In that case, three men committed a murder. Police initially interviewed several suspects, including the defendant, but were not able to bring charges at that time. Later, after a DNA analysis provided further evidence of the defendant's involvement, the defendant agreed to another voluntary interview. The interview lasted several hours and the defendant was repeatedly confronted with the DNA evidence and other indicia of his guilt, and advised to "get on the bus" and "cooperate"[3] in order to advantage himself in what could be a capital case.

---

1. *See generally* S.L. 2017-57, § 16D.4.
2. ___ N.C. App. ___, 795 S.E.2d 625, *review granted*, ___ N.C. ___, 798 S.E.2d 525 (2017).
3. *Id.* at ___, 795 S.E.2d at 630.

The court of appeals determined that the defendant's eventual statements were involuntary in light of all the circumstances:

> Defendant was questioned for hours after he should have been *Mirandized* [but was not, though he was given *Miranda* warnings before his most incriminating statements] and, throughout this questioning, the detectives repeatedly told Defendant they knew he was lying; that they had DNA proof of Defendant's guilt; that only a guilty person would have known [the victim] was shot in the back of the neck; that this could be a capital case, and that Defendant's treatment would depend on his cooperation; that the district attorney's office would usually work with those who cooperated; that [one of the officers] would consider testifying on Defendant's behalf; that Defendant would feel better if he confessed and did right by God and his children; and that Defendant should get the "best seat on the bus" by giving statements against the two other men involved. It is also clear that the detectives decided to arrest Defendant [partway through the interview] in order to shake him up.[4]

A number of the officers' statements were at odds with the recommendations in the main text regarding statements officers should avoid making to defendants. Problematic statements in this case include the suggestion that an officer might testify on the defendant's behalf and the suggestion of leniency if the defendant were to make a statement—e.g., by referring to the district attorney's willingness to work with the defendant who has the "best seat" on the "bus." At the time of this writing, the North Carolina Supreme Court has agreed to review this case.

## The *Miranda* Rule and Additional Statutory Rights (page 570)

### Overview (page 570)

#### A Young Arrestee's Additional Statutory Warnings and Rights (page 572)

There has been considerable litigation concerning the statutory rights of young arrestees since the publication of the main text. In *State v. Benitez*,[5] the court ruled that a "guardian" is a relationship that must be established through a "legal process." In other words, an adult is not a "guardian" of a young person simply because the two are related (in *Benitez*, the adult was the child's uncle) and live together, and the adult takes care of the young person's needs such as food, shelter, and school enrollment.

In *State v. Saldierna*,[6] the court ruled that a juvenile who wants to assert his or her right to have a parent, guardian, or custodian present must do so unambiguously, just as an adult arrestee who wants to assert his or her *Miranda* rights must do so unambiguously. The case involved a 16-year-old's question, "Um, can I call my mom?" The state supreme court ruled that the remark was "at best an ambiguous invocation of his right to have his mother present"[7] that did not require officers to cease questioning or even seek clarification regarding the juvenile's wishes.

---

4. *Id.* at ___, 795 S.E.2d at 639.
5. ___ N.C. App. ___, 813 S.E.2d 268 (2018).
6. 369 N.C. 401 (2016).
7. *Id.* at 409.

### When the *Miranda* Rule Applies: Custody and Interrogation (page 573)
#### *The Meaning of "Custody"* (page 573)
##### The seizure of a person under the Fourth Amendment (page 574)

Additional recent cases illustrating that not every seizure amounts to custody include *State v. Burris*[8] and *State v. Barnes.*[9]

##### NEW SECTION: Person subject to involuntary commitment

A person confined under a civil commitment order may be considered in custody for *Miranda* purposes, at least under certain circumstances. In *State v. Hammonds*, the court ruled that the defendant was in custody while "confined under a civil commitment order."[10] He was a suspect in an armed robbery, but shortly after the robbery, as a result of a drug overdose, he was confined at a hospital based upon a magistrate's determination that he was "mentally ill and dangerous to self or others."[11] Officers questioned him about the robbery without informing him of his *Miranda* rights, and he made incriminating statements. His motion to suppress was denied by the trial court, but the state supreme court ultimately reversed. It noted that the defendant's freedom of movement was severely restricted by the civil commitment order, that the officers failed to inform him he was free to terminate the questioning, and that the officers indicated they would leave only after he spoke to them about the robbery. The court ruled that, considering all the circumstances, "these statements, made to a suspect whose freedom is already severely restricted because of an involuntary commitment, would lead a reasonable person in this position to believe 'he was not at liberty to terminate the interrogation' without first answering his interrogators' questions about his suspected criminal activity."[12]

### Waiver of *Miranda* Rights (page 578)

A recent North Carolina case finding an implied waiver is *State v. Knight*,[13] where the defendant was read his *Miranda* rights, then talked at length with the officers without expressly acknowledging or waiving his rights. The state supreme court, applying *Berghuis v. Thompkins*,[14] found that there was no *Miranda* violation, as the defendant understood his *Miranda* rights and effected an implied waiver by choosing to speak with the officers. The court specifically rejected the idea that an express acknowledgment, statement of understanding, or waiver was required, instead applying a totality of the circumstances analysis.

# Part II. Lineups and Other Identification Procedures (page 594)

## Introduction (page 594)
### Juveniles (page 594)

Regarding what age renders a suspect a juvenile for purposes of conducting nontestimonial identification procedures, see page 46 of this supplement.

---

8. ___ N.C. App. ___, 799 S.E.2d 452 (2017) (ruling that the defendant was not in custody for *Miranda* purposes just because an officer had detained the defendant and was in possession of the defendant's driver's license).

9. ___ N.C. App. ___, 789 S.E.2d. 488 (2016) (ruling that although the defendant was detained in handcuffs at the time he was questioned, he was not, based on the totality of the circumstances, "in custody" for purposes of *Miranda*; the handcuffs were used for "officer safety" while a parole officer searched the defendant's cousin's house).

10. 370 N.C. 158, 159 (2017).

11. *Id.*

12. *Id.* at 166 (citation omitted).

13. ___ N.C. ___, 799 S.E.2d 603 (2017).

14. 560 U.S. 370 (2010).

## Nonsuggestiveness of the Identification Procedure under
## Due Process Clause (page 595)

Although most of the cases concerning suggestive identification procedures involve field identification procedures conducted by officers, in *State v. Malone*[15] the court ruled that eyewitness identifications were tainted by a trial preparation meeting between two eyewitnesses and a legal assistant from the district attorney's office. The legal assistant showed the witnesses photographs of the defendant, a surveillance video of the crime scene, and part of the defendant's recorded interview with police officers, among other items. Although at the time of the crime, neither witness was able to give detailed descriptions of the defendant or positively identify him, they identified him at trial. The court stated: "It is likely the witnesses would assume [the legal assistant] showed them the photographs and videos because the individuals portrayed therein were suspected of being guilty."[16] This process was impermissibly suggestive and tainted the witnesses' in-court identification of the defendant. At the time of this writing, the North Carolina Supreme Court has agreed to review this case.

## North Carolina Statutory Procedures for Live Lineups and Photo Lineups (page 598)

On page 598 of the main text, in footnote 169, the citation to S.L. 2007-434 should instead be to S.L. 2007-421.

---

15. ___ N.C. App. ___, 807 S.E.2d 639 (2017), *review allowed*, ___ N.C. ___, 809 S.E.2d 586 (2018).
16. *Id* at ___, 807 S.E.2d at 650.

# Chapter 5 Appendix: Case Summaries

# I. Interrogation and Confessions (page 609)

## Voluntariness of the Defendant's Statement (page 609)
### Generally (page 609)
**NORTH CAROLINA COURT OF APPEALS** (page 610)

*State v. Johnson*, ___ N.C. App. ___, 795 S.E.2d. 625, *review granted*, ___ N.C. ___, 798 S.E.2d 525 (2017). Three men committed a murder. Police interviewed several suspects, including the defendant, but were unable to bring charges at that time. Later, after a DNA analysis provided further evidence of the defendant's involvement, the defendant agreed to another voluntary interview. The interview lasted several hours and the defendant was repeatedly confronted with the DNA evidence and other indicia of his guilt, and advised to "get on the bus" and "cooperate" in order to advantage himself in what could be a capital case. The court of appeals determined that the defendant's eventual statements were involuntary in light of all the circumstances:

> Defendant was questioned for hours after he should have been *Mirandized* [but was not, though he was given *Miranda* warnings before his most incriminating statements] and, throughout this questioning, the detectives repeatedly told Defendant they knew he was lying; that they had DNA proof of Defendant's guilt; that only a guilty person would have known [the victim] was shot in the back of the neck; that this could be a capital case, and that Defendant's treatment would depend on his cooperation; that the district attorney's office would usually work with those who cooperated; that [one of the officers] would consider testifying on Defendant's behalf; that Defendant would feel better if he confessed and did right by God and his children; and that Defendant should get the "best seat on the bus" by giving statements against the two other men involved. It is also clear that the detectives decided to arrest Defendant [partway through the interview] in order to shake him up.

However, the court ruled that the error was harmless beyond a reasonable doubt in light of the overwhelming evidence of the defendant's guilt. At the time of this writing, the North Carolina Supreme Court has agreed to review this case.

## Defendant's Statements: *Miranda* Warnings and Waiver (page 616)
### Waiver of *Miranda* Rights (page 621)
### *Generally* (page 621)
**NORTH CAROLINA COURT OF APPEALS** (page 624)

*State v. Knight*, ___ N.C. ___, 799 S.E.2d 603 (2017). The defendant was arrested for rape, and officers read him his *Miranda* rights. He did not expressly acknowledge or waive them, but talked at length with the officers, attempting to convince them of his innocence but in fact making statements that eventually became part of the State's case against him. He moved to suppress the statements prior to trial but his motion was denied. After he was convicted, he appealed. The court of appeals found a *Miranda* violation because the defendant did not expressly waive his rights, though a majority of the court saw it as harmless. The state supreme court, applying *Berghuis v. Thompkins*, 560 U.S. 370 (2010), found that there was no *Miranda* violation, as the defendant understood his *Miranda* rights and effected an implied waiver by choosing to speak with the officers.

The court noted that the defendant was an adult who spoke English fluently and had his rights read to him, so there was no doubt that he understood them. And it rejected the idea that an express acknowledgment, statement of understanding, or waiver was required, instead applying a totality of the circumstances analysis.

*State v. Santillan*, ___ N.C. App. ___, ___ S.E.2d ___, 2018 WL 2011058 (May 1, 2018). Police arrested a 15-year-old suspect in connection with a double murder. He initially waived his right to counsel, but later asserted it, leading the officers to stop questioning him. He then had a brief exchange with the chief of police in which, among other things, the chief told him that he had "f***** up." The defendant subsequently waived his right to counsel again and made further statements. His motion to suppress those statements was denied and they were admitted against him at trial. The court of appeals remanded for further findings regarding whether the conversation with the chief was an unlawful attempt to interrogate an arrestee who had asserted his right to counsel. The court rejected the defendant's argument that "his second waiver [of his right to counsel] was involuntary because of factors including his young age, the officers' interrogation tactics, and his lack of sleep, food, and medication." The court agreed with the trial judge that the defendant's "actions and statements show[ed] awareness and cognitive reasoning during the entire interview" and that the defendant "was not coerced into making any statements, but rather made his statements voluntarily."

## The Meaning of "Custody" under *Miranda* (page 630)
### Generally (page 630)
**NORTH CAROLINA SUPREME COURT** (page 633)

*State v. Hammonds*, 370 N.C. 158 (2017). The defendant was in custody for *Miranda* purposes while "confined under a civil commitment order." He was a suspect in an armed robbery, but shortly after the robbery, as a result of a drug overdose, he was confined at a hospital based upon a magistrate's determination that he was "mentally ill and dangerous to self or others." Officers questioned him about the robbery without informing him of his *Miranda* rights, and he made incriminating statements. His motion to suppress was denied by the trial court, but the state supreme court ultimately reversed. It noted that the defendant's freedom of movement was severely restricted by the civil commitment order, that the officers failed to inform him that he was free to terminate the questioning, and that the officers indicated they would leave only after he spoke to them about the robbery. The court ruled that, considering all the circumstances, "these statements, made to a suspect whose freedom is already severely restricted because of an involuntary commitment, would lead a reasonable person in this position to believe he 'was not at liberty to terminate the interrogation' without first answering his interrogators' questions about his suspected criminal activity." For a more complete discussion of *Hammonds*, see Bob Farb, *New North Carolina Appellate Cases on the Meaning of Custody under* Miranda v. Arizona, UNC SCH. OF GOV'T: N.C. CRIM. L. BLOG (June 14, 2016), https://nccriminallaw.sog.unc.edu/new-north-carolina-appellate-cases-meaning-custody-miranda-v-arizona/.

**NORTH CAROLINA COURT OF APPEALS**

*State v. Parlier*, ___ N.C. App. ___, 797 S.E.2d 340 (2017). In this child sexual assault case, the court rejected the defendant's argument that his confession was obtained in violation of *Miranda*. During an interview at the sheriff's department, the defendant admitted that he had had sex with the victim. The transcript and videotape of the interview was admitted at trial. The court rejected the defendant's argument that a custodial interrogation occurred. The defendant contacted a detective investigating the case and voluntarily traveled to the sheriff's department. After the detective invited the defendant to speak with her, the defendant followed her to an interview room. The defendant was not handcuffed or restrained and the interview room door and hallway doors were unlocked. The defendant neither asked to leave nor expressed any reservations about speaking with the detective. A reasonable person in the defendant's position would not have understood this to be a custodial interrogation.

*State v. Portillo*, ___ N.C. App. ___, 787 S.E.2d 822 (2016). The defendant was injured when, in the course of robbing and murdering a victim, the victim shot back and wounded the defendant. He was taken to the hospital where he remained under officers' guard. The next day, investigators arrived to question him. He made incriminating statements that he later moved to suppress based on the fact that he had not been read his *Miranda* rights. The court of appeals determined that he was not in custody for *Miranda* purposes. His movement was restrained primarily by his medical condition rather than by the police, and he had not been arrested or even handcuffed. The fact that officers suspected him of the crime and may have intended to arrest him was not dispositive.

*State v. Barnes*, ___ N.C. App. ___, 789 S.E.2d. 488 (2016). Although the defendant was in handcuffs at the time of the questioning, he was not, based on the totality of the circumstances, "in custody" for purposes of *Miranda*. While the defendant was visiting his cousin's house, a parole officer arrived to search the cousin's home. The parole officer recognized the defendant as a probationer and the officer advised him that he was also subject to a warrantless search because of his status. The officer put the defendant in handcuffs "for officer safety" and seated the two men on the front porch while officers conducted a search. During the search, the parole officer found a jacket with what appeared to be crack cocaine inside a pocket. The officer asked the defendant and his cousin to identify the owner of the jacket. The defendant claimed the jacket and was charged with a drug offense. The court held: "Based on the totality of circumstances, we conclude that a reasonable person in Defendant's situation, though in handcuffs would not believe his restraint rose to the level of the restraint associated with a formal arrest." The court noted that the regular conditions of probation include the requirement that a probationer submit to warrantless searches. Also, the defendant was informed that he would be placed in handcuffs for officer safety and he was never told that his detention was anything other than temporary. Further, the court reasoned, "as a probationer subject to random searches as a condition of probation, Defendant would objectively understand the purpose of the restraints and the fact that the period of restraint was for a temporary duration." For a more complete discussion of *Barnes*, see Bob Farb, *Court of Appeals Rules That Probationer Was Not in Custody When Handcuffed for Safety Reasons*, UNC Sch. of Gov't: N.C. Crim. L. Blog (July 26, 2016), https://nccriminallaw.sog.unc.edu/court-appeals-rules-probationer-not-custody-handcuffed-safety-reasons/.

## Traffic Cases (page 643)

### NORTH CAROLINA COURT OF APPEALS (page 645)

*State v. Burris*, ___ N.C. App. ___, 799 S.E.2d 452 (2017). The defendant was not in custody for *Miranda* purposes just because an officer had detained the defendant and was in possession of the defendant's driver's license. The matter arose when an officer responded to a suspicious person call at a hotel and found the defendant in the driver's seat of a vehicle parked under an overhang. The officer smelled an odor of alcohol, and was also concerned about similarities to a robbery that had recently occurred at a nearby hotel. Accordingly, he asked the defendant for identification, then held the defendant's license and instructed the defendant to "hold tight." During the resulting detention, the defendant admitted to driving the vehicle, a fact that became important when he was eventually charged with DWI. He moved to suppress, arguing that he had been subjected to custodial interrogation without being given his *Miranda* warnings. Both the trial judge and the court of appeals disagreed, with the latter noting that the defendant had erroneously conflated the *Miranda* custody standard (whether the suspect has been restrained to a degree associated with an arrest) with the standard for a seizure (whether the suspect is free to leave). Here, the defendant was standing outside of his own vehicle while speaking with the detective. He was not handcuffed or told he was under arrest, and other than his license being retained, his movement was not stopped or limited further. No mention of any possible suspicion of the defendant being involved in criminal activity, impaired driving or otherwise, had yet been made. A reasonable person in these circumstances would not have believed that he or she was under arrest at the time.

## The Meaning of "Interrogation" under *Miranda* (page 650)
### Volunteered Statements (page 655)
#### NORTH CAROLINA COURT OF APPEALS (page 656)

*State v. Moore*, ___ N.C. App. ___, 803 S.E.2d 196 (2017). The trial court did not err by denying the defendant's motion to suppress statements made to an officer while the officer was transporting the defendant to the law enforcement center. It was undisputed that the defendant made the inculpatory statements while in custody and before he had been given his *Miranda* rights. However, the court held that the defendant was not subjected to interrogation; rather, his statements were spontaneous utterances. This was so even though the statements followed a supervising officer's radio communication with the transporting officer in which the supervisor asked the transporting officer whether the defendant had said anything about the location of the vehicle involved in the incident. This "brief exchange between two law enforcement officers" was not directed at the defendant, was not the functional equivalent of an interrogation, and did not call for an incriminating response.

*State v. Burton*, ___ N.C. App. ___, 796 S.E.2d 65 (2017). The defendant and another man were arrested in connection with the possession of marijuana and cocaine in a vehicle. The arresting officer obtained charges against both individuals, then read the arrest warrants to each arrestee in the other's presence. The defendant told the officer that the other individual should not be charged with possession of the cocaine because it was the defendant's. That statement was not obtained in violation of *Miranda*—reading the arrest warrants aloud was not "interrogation." Arresting officers must inform arrestees of the charges against them, and the defendant failed to show that reading the charges in the presence of both arrestees was designed to elicit an incriminating response.

## North Carolina Statutory Warnings for Young Arrestees (page 684)
#### NORTH CAROLINA SUPREME COURT (page 684)

*State v. Saldierna*, 369 N.C. 401 (2016). Officers arrested a 16-year-old juvenile in connection with several break-ins and sought to question him. The juvenile was advised of, and signed a waiver of, his *Miranda* rights and his statutory right to have a parent or guardian present. Shortly thereafter, he asked, "Um, can I call my mom?" An officer allowed him to use a phone, but he was unable to reach his mother. The interview resumed, and the juvenile admitted involvement. He later moved to suppress, contending that his request to call his mother amounted to an assertion of his right to have a parent present. The motion was denied by the trial judge. The court of appeals reversed, concluding that the question was ambiguous but that, unlike in the *Miranda* context, an officer should clarify ambiguous comments regarding juvenile rights. The state supreme court reversed again, ruling that the juvenile's remark was "at best an ambiguous invocation of his right to have his mother present," and applying *Miranda* precedent in holding that "without an unambiguous, unequivocal invocation of defendant's right [to have a parent or guardian present] law enforcement officers had no duty to ask clarifying questions or to cease questioning." The court remanded the matter to the court of appeals to review whether the juvenile's waiver of his rights was knowing and voluntary. For a more complete discussion of *Saldierna*, see Bob Farb, *North Carolina Supreme Court Rules That Juvenile's Request to Call Mother During Custodial Interrogation Was Not Clear Invocation of Statutory Right to Consult a Parent or Guardian to Bar Further Interrogation*, UNC Sch. of Gov't: N.C. Crim. L. Blog (Feb. 28, 2017), https://nccriminallaw.sog.unc.edu/2017/02/.

**NORTH CAROLINA COURT OF APPEALS** (page 684)

**State v. Benitez**, ___ N.C. App. ___, 813 S.E. 2d 268 (2018). The 13-year-old defendant was questioned in the presence of his uncle, with whom he lived, and admitted shooting a victim in the head. Two weeks later, the court appointed DSS as a guardian for the defendant because he had appeared in court with no family, his mother was believed to be in El Salvador, and his father's whereabouts were unknown. The defendant eventually pled guilty to first-degree murder, and later filed an MAR, alleging that his trial counsel had provided ineffective assistance by failing to move to suppress the statement as obtained in violation of the defendant's statutory right to have a parent or guardian present. The attorney indicated that he had researched the issue but concluded that the uncle qualified as a guardian under existing case law given that the juvenile had lived with him for more than a year, that he met the juvenile's needs, and that he signed paperwork for school and otherwise as the defendant's guardian. Although *State v. Oglesby*, 361 N.C. 550 (2007) (finding that a juvenile's aunt was not a guardian and stating that only a "legal process" could render a person a guardian), was perhaps to the contrary, the precise scope and meaning of *Oglesby* was not clear at the time and counsel's decision not to pursue the issue based on the research he had done was not unreasonable. As a second issue, the defendant argued that his waiver of his right to remain silent was not knowing, voluntary, and intelligent. The court of appeals remanded that issue for further findings by the trial court, noting a lack of findings regarding the defendant's "experience, education, background, and intelligence." The court appeared to be especially concerned with suggestions in the record that the defendant suffered from some mental disease or defect, perhaps an intellectual disability.

**State v. Saldierna**, ___ N.C. App. ___, 803 S.E.2d 33, *review granted*, ___ N.C. ___, 805 S.E.2d 482 (2017). The basic facts of this case are set forth in the summary of a prior proceeding in the same matter (see page 62). In addition, the officer who questioned the juvenile gave him rights forms in English and in Spanish, but the juvenile signed only the English version of the form. On remand from the state supreme court, the court of appeals ruled that the juvenile did not knowingly, willingly, and understandingly waive his rights. He had only an eighth-grade education and Spanish was his primary language. He could write in English, but had difficulty reading English and understanding spoken English. The transcript of the audio recording in which the defendant was said to have waived his rights revealed that the detective spoke to the defendant entirely in English and that the defendant gave several "[unintelligible]" responses or non-responses to the detective's questions pertaining to whether he understood his rights. There was no indication that the defendant had any familiarity with the criminal justice system and the record indicates that the defendant might not have fully understood the detective's questions. The court "decline[d] to give any weight to recitals, like the juvenile rights waiver form signed by defendant, which merely formalize constitutional requirements." It added that "a waiver should be voluntary, not just on its face, i.e., the paper it is written on, but in fact. It should be unequivocal and unassailable when the subject is a juvenile." And it emphasized that the defendant sought to call his mother before speaking with the officers, which is consistent with a lack of understanding of the situation and how best to proceed. As of this writing, the state supreme court has agreed to review this case.

**State v. Watson**, ___ N.C. App. ___, 792 S.E.2d 171 (2016). The defendant was 16 years old when he was arrested for robbery. An officer advised him of his juvenile rights and the defendant agreed to speak with the officer. However, the juvenile filled out the form indicating that his mother was present, rather than indicating that he did not wish for her to be present. He then made incriminating statements. The trial court found that the form had been filled out in "error," but that there was no indication that the defendant wanted his mother to be present. The court of appeals affirmed, agreeing that the form was completed inaccurately and that the defendant had not requested his mother be present. For a more complete discussion of *Watson*, see Bob Farb, *North Carolina Court of Appeals Finds That Erroneous Completion of Juvenile Waiver of Rights Form Did Not Bar Admissibility of Confession*, UNC Sch. of Gov't: N.C. Crim. L. Blog (Oct. 25, 2016), https://nccriminallaw.sog.unc.edu/north-carolina-court-appeals-finds-erroneous-completion-juvenile-waiver-rights-form-not-bar-admissibility-confession/.

# II. Lineups and Other Identification Procedures (page 709)

## Due Process Review of Identification Procedures (page 710)

### Generally (page 710)

**NORTH CAROLINA COURT OF APPEALS** (page 712)

*State v. Malone,* ___ N.C. App. ___, 807 S.E.2d 639 (2017) *review allowed,* ___ N.C. ___, 809 S.E.2d 586 (2018). The court held that identification procedures used with respect to two eyewitnesses to a murder, Alvarez and Lopez, violated Due Process. At issue was a meeting between the two eyewitnesses and a legal assistant from the district attorney's office. The legal assistant met with the eyewitnesses and showed them: photographs of the defendant and another individual who already had been convicted for his role in the shooting; a surveillance video, taken from a security camera where the incident occurred; and part of the defendant's recorded interview with police officers. While the eyewitnesses were watching the interview, Alvarez was standing near a window and happened to see the defendant exiting a police car. Alvarez directed Lopez to look outside and she too saw the defendant exiting the police car, wearing an orange jumpsuit, in handcuffs, and escorted by an officer. The evidence at trial showed that after the shooting neither Lopez nor Alvarez were able to give detailed descriptions of the defendant or positively identify him. Then, three and a half years later, and approximately two weeks prior to trial, the witnesses met with the legal assistant and viewed the materials described above. The court stated: "It is likely the witnesses would assume [the legal assistant] showed them the photographs and videos because the individuals portrayed therein were suspected of being guilty." This process was impermissibly suggestive. And it tainted the witnesses' in-court identifications of the defendant, which were not likely of independent origin given the short amount of time the witnesses had to view the defendant during the crime, their inability to positively identify him two days after the incident, and their inconsistent descriptions of him. The court went on to hold that admission of the identification testimony was not harmless beyond a reasonable doubt and reversed. However, it rejected the defendant's argument that the legal assistant subjected Lopez and Alvarez to an impermissible show up procedure. Specifically, it found that there was no evidence to support the defendant's argument that the witnesses' looking out of the window at the exact moment the defendant exited a police car was coordinated by the legal assistant to have the witnesses view the defendant in person. For a more complete discussion of *Malone,* see Jeff Welty, *Trial Preparation Taints Eyewitnesses' In-Court Identification, Leads to Reversal of Murder Conviction,* UNC SCH. OF GOV'T: N.C. CRIM. L. BLOG (Nov. 20, 2017), https://nccriminallaw.sog.unc.edu/trial-preparation-taints-eyewitnesses-court-identification-leads-reversal-murder-conviction/. As of this writing, the North Carolina Supreme Court has agreed to review this case.

## Statutory Procedures Involving Lineups (page 714)

**NORTH CAROLINA COURT OF APPEALS** (page 714)

On page 715, the main volume summarizes *State v. Boozer.* The correct citation for that case is 210 N.C. App. 371 (2011), not 210 N.C. App. 391 (2011).

# Case and Statute Index

## Cases

### A

Arizona v. Gant, 556 U.S. 332 (2009) *39*

### B

Berghuis v. Thompkins, 560 U.S. 370 (2010) *57, 59*
Birchfield v. North Dakota, 579 U.S. ___, 136 S. Ct. 2160 (2016) *29, 37*
Brown v. Texas, 443 U.S. 47 (1979) *20*
Byrd v. United States, 584 U.S. ___, 138 S. Ct. 1518 (2018) *25, 26*

### C

Carpenter v. United States, ___ U.S. ___, 138 S. Ct. 2206 (2018) *26, 27, 33*
Collins v. Virginia, 584 U.S. ___, 138 S. Ct. 1663 (2018) *28, 32, 35*

### D

Davis v. Town of Southern Pines, 116 N.C. App. 663 (1994) *2*
District of Columbia v. Wesby, 583 U.S. ___, 138 S. Ct. 577 (2018) *5, 21*

### F

Florida v. Royer, 460 U.S. 491 (1983) *28*

### H

Heien v. North Carolina, 135 S. Ct. 530 (2014) *3, 14*

### M

Missouri v. McNeely, 569 U.S. 141 (2013) *37*

### N

Navarette v. California, 134 S. Ct. 1683 (2014) *4*

### R

Riley v. California, 573 U.S. ___, 134 S. Ct. 2473 (2014) *25, 31*
Rodriguez v. United States, 575 U.S. ___, 135 S. Ct. 1609 (2015) *6, 7, 15, 18, 26*

### S

State v. Adams, ___ N.C. App. ___, 794 S.E.2d 357 (2016) *9, 23*
State v. Allman, 369 N.C. 292 (2016) *44, 50*
State v. Ashworth, ___ N.C. App. ___, 790 S.E.2d 173 (2016) *20*
State v. Barnes, ___ N.C. App. ___, 789 S.E.2d. 488 (2016) *57, 61*
State v. Benitez, ___ N.C. App. ___, 813 S.E.2d 268 (2018) *56, 63*
State v. Benters, 367 N.C. 660 (2014) *43*
State v. Blankenship, 230 N.C. App. 113 (2013) *4*
State v. Boozer, 210 N.C. App. 371 (2011) *64*
State v. Brody, ___ N.C. App. ___, 796 S.E.2d 384 (2017) *43, 49*
State v. Bullock, 370 N.C. 256 (2017) *6, 7, 8, 15, 18, 19*
State v. Bullock, ___ N.C. App. ___, 785 S.E.2d 746 (2016) *15*
State v. Bullock, ___ N.C. App. ___, 811 S.E.2d 713 (2018) *18, 34*
State v. Burris, ___ N.C. App. ___, 799 S.E.2d 452 (2017) *29, 37, 57, 61*
State v. Burton, ___ N.C. App. ___, 796 S.E.2d. 65 (2017) *36, 62*
State v. Burwell, ___ N.C. App. ___, 808 S.E.2d 583 (2017) *2, 20, 53*
State v. Campola, ___ N.C. App. ___, 812 S.E.2d 681 (2018) *7, 17*
State v. Clapp, ___ N.C. App. ___, ___ S.E.2d ___, WL 2626889 (June 5, 2018) *21*
State v. Cobb, ___ N.C. App. ___, 789 S.E.2d 532 (2016) *34*
State v. Cox, ___ N.C. App. ___, ___ S.E.2d ___, WL 2207337 (May 15, 2018) *7, 16*
State v. Daniel, ___ N.C. App. ___, 814 S.E.2d 618 (2018) *22*
State v. Downey, 370 N.C. 507 (2018) *7, 15*
State v. Downey, ___ N.C. App. ___, 791 S.E.2d 257 (2016) *41, 53*
State v. Downey, ___ N.C. App. ___, 796 S.E.2d 517 (2017) *15*
State v. Eldridge, ___ N.C. App. ___, 790 S.E.2d 740 (2016) *3, 14*
State v. Evans, ___ N.C. App. ___, 795 S.E.2d 444 (2017) *13*

## Statutes

### North Carolina General Statues

### North Carolina Session Laws

### Federal Statutes